STILL WATERS,
Exploring America's

By Ron Fisher
Photographed by Sam Abell

WHITE WATERS
Rivers and Lakes

Prepared by the Special Publications Division
National Geographic Society, Washington, D. C.

STILL WATERS, WHITE WATERS
By Ron Fisher, *National Geographic Staff*
Photographed by Sam Abell

Published by
THE NATIONAL GEOGRAPHIC SOCIETY
ROBERT E. DOYLE, *President*
MELVILLE BELL GROSVENOR, *Editor Emeritus*
GILBERT M. GROSVENOR, *Editor*

Prepared by
THE SPECIAL PUBLICATIONS DIVISION
ROBERT L. BREEDEN, *Editor*
DONALD J. CRUMP, *Associate Editor*
PHILIP B. SILCOTT, *Senior Editor*
MARY ANN HARRELL, *Managing Editor*
TONI EUGENE, *Senior Researcher;* ELIZABETH C.
    WAGNER, PEGGY D. WINSTON, *Researchers*

Illustrations and Design
DAVID R. BRIDGE, *Picture Editor*
DON A. SPARKS, *Assistant Picture Editor*
URSULA PERRIN VOSSELER, *Art Director*
SUEZ B. KEHL, *Assistant Art Director*
CHRISTINE K. ECKSTROM, JUDITH GREEN, TEE
    LOFTIN, LOUISA MAGZANIAN, TOM MELHAM,
    EDWARD O. WELLES, JR., *Picture Legends*
JOHN D. GARST, JR., PETER J. BALCH,
    CHARLES W. BERRY, MARGARET A. DEANE,
    Map Research, Design, and Production
ROLAND DesCOMBES, *Drawings*

Production and Printing
ROBERT W. MESSER, *Production Manager*
GEORGE V. WHITE, *Assistant Production Manager*
RAJA D. MURSHED, JUNE L. GRAHAM, CHRISTINE
    A. ROBERTS, *Production Assistants*
JOHN R. METCALFE, *Engraving and Printing*
DEBRA A. ANTONINI, JANE H. BUXTON, ALICIA
    L. DIFFENDERFFER, SUZANNE J. JACOBSON, CLEO
    PETROFF, KATHERYN M. SLOCUM, SUZANNE
    VENINO, MARILYN L. WILBUR, *Staff Assistants*
BRIT AABAKKEN PETERSON, *Index*

Library of Congress ℂℙ Data: page 199

*Overleaf: Canoeist Craig Lockwood rides the crest of a wave in Coal
Creek Rapid on the Green River in Utah, where the author's party
faced its roughest water. Page 1: An angler releases a cutthroat trout
he hooked in Yellowstone Lake. Endpapers: Maine's Allagash
Wilderness Waterway offers calm reaches of lake and pond in its
southern portion—excitement and speed in the nine-mile course
through Chase Rapids. Bookbinding: Paddles used by the author and
the photographer derive from northeastern Indian models.*

ENDPAPERS: NATIONAL GEOGRAPHIC PHOTOGRAPHER STEVE RAYMER
BOOKBINDING DESIGN: CHARLES W. BERRY

*Steering his wood-and-canvas canoe beneath
a bridge, author Ron Fisher glides toward
the shore of Maine's Churchill Lake—
late in the year but early in his 12-month
journey canoeing America's lakes and rivers.*

Foreword

My first impression of canoeing was from the vantage point of a row-boat. I was ten. A friend and I were merrily hacking—mostly in circles—around a summer-camp lake in Michigan. From far behind us, someone hollered, "Hey! You want to race?" No one was visible, nor could we see the bulky aluminum reflection from a rowboat. They yelled again; we focused on the sound and saw twin spots of light flash, fade, flash again: wet, wooden paddles. A canoe!

Our boat clanked toward shore, the two of us bellowing cadence and encouragement at each other. All too often one of us would stroke, miss the water completely, and smack the boat with a resounding, numbing roundhouse. By the time we reached the swimmers' platform a hundred feet from the beach, we were ahead, but not by much. We chose a course wide of the platform and its low diving board. The canoeists sped straight ahead, ducked under the diving board, pivoted past the platform, and coasted into shallow water, the winners.

Now this scene reminds me of that described by John McPhee in *The Survival of the Bark Canoe*—when Indians first met white men: "...here were bark canoes on big rivers and ocean bays curiously circling ships from another world. Longboats were lowered, to be rowed by crews of four and upward. The sailors hauled at their oars. The Indians, two to a canoe, indolently whisked their narrow paddles and easily drew away. In their wake they left a stunning impression. Not only were they faster. They could see where they were going."

Four hundred years later the Indians and their wilderness are largely gone, tamed in part by canoes which explorers used to penetrate their new world. Today, for pleasure and to escape from the contemporary world, people by the thousand choose to canoe.

They are drawn to it for some of the reasons Ron Fisher and I were. It seems do-able, a straightforward and delightful way to approach nature. It is, of course, harder than it looks, and demands skill and common sense.

Canoeing is, above all, gratifying to the senses. In its noiseless atmosphere, the steady sounds are of wind and water, the occasional sounds are of animals. There is rarely enough to eat, Ron tells me; food tastes best out-of-doors. And for touch there is a wooden paddle and with it the powerful satisfaction of propelling yourself across the water.

During our year afloat Ron and I canoed more than 1,600 miles on all manner of waters. At the end we were not experts—which we should have been to canoe parts of the Green River—but we were competent. Canoeing inspires humility: We were always the lowest object on the landscape, often vulnerable to water and weather, and, at the beginning, badly in need of guides. But at the end, alone at night on a corner of the Arctic Ocean, we had confidence in our canoes and in ourselves. And we were friends. Canoeing, a two-person pastime, had made it so.

SAM ABELL

Live oaks filmy with Spanish moss surround a campsite near Suwannee Springs, Florida, as the author crouches by his evening fire to boil macaroni. Ron paddled 230 miles on the serpentine Suwannee River, between Georgia's Okefenokee Swamp and the Gulf of

Contents

*Mexico — and recalls, "In eleven days
of floating down the Suwannee,
we saw no canoes but our own."*

1

Loon Songs
in the
Northern Woods

I TOOK PART IN A LAUNCHING A WHILE BACK. It was cheerful, and matter-of-fact. Two new canoes — we called them *I'm OK* and *You're OK* — slipped gracefully into the lapping blue shallows along Rainy Lake, just east of International Falls, Minnesota. They were wood-and-canvas "Guide" models, made by Old Town in Maine. Their varnished white-cedar ribs caught the light and batted it at me, and water beaded their forest-green sides as they rocked in the wavelets.

The summer was ending as our party began a trip across Minnesota. We were headed for Grand Portage, 275 miles away on Lake Superior. We would have Canada on our left and the United States on our right; our route would follow the border exactly. We would pass south of Ontario's Quetico Provincial Park, a million acres of lakes and forests; and, in the U. S., we would paddle along the edges of Voyageurs National Park to the million-acre, thousand-lake Boundary Waters Canoe Area, a canoeist's wilderness within Superior National Forest. All together, the area is some of the finest canoeing country in North America, if not in the world.

We loaded the canoes with canvas packs stuffed with food and camping equipment sufficient for three weeks. There were six of us in three canoes, and about midday we pushed off. Rollers — a few tipped with white — hurried beneath us as we began paddling down Rainy Lake. It was slow going at first, as I practiced synchronizing my strokes with Mike Lande, my partner. A far more experienced canoeist than I, Mike kept me busy with instructions and pointers: the best grip for my paddle, the proper depth for my stroke, how to make my shoulders and back do the work, how to feather my paddle.

"Turn it so the blade is horizontal to the water and the wind

Treading a path worn smooth by generations of Indians, explorers, and voyageurs, guide John Bartholomew lugs his wood-and-canvas canoe along the Grand Portage Trail. October leaves carpet the nine-mile track that links Lake Superior to Minnesota's Boundary Waters Canoe Area.

9

when you complete a stroke," he said. "With the wind this strong, every bit of resistance hurts us."

As the afternoon wore on and we crept down the lake, the paddling became automatic and the rocking of the canoe hypnotic. It was in sharp contrast to the hurried drive photographer Sam Abell and I had just made from Washington, D. C., with our canoes bottom-up on our van and long-necked signs rising above the interchanges: "Next Exit," "Last Oasis," "Second Right."

That first day on Rainy Lake we didn't get very far. What with the late start and the wind snapping the collar of my jacket and building a few whitecaps, we stopped after only a few miles and camped on Dryweed Island. As it turned out, we would stay there for two days, wind-bound before we had hardly begun.

But Rainy is a big lake, with several miles of exposed water where the wind has a chance to build waves bigger than canoes should venture into. It was on this lake that a couple of young men drowned a few years back, caught in the middle in a sudden wind. So we stayed put, built a makeshift shelter to keep the drizzle off, waited for the weather to clear, and got acquainted.

Mike Lande, a young outfitter on Gunflint Trail, gave up a career as a chemist in Minneapolis to come to the wilderness. He was impervious to the cold; our second morning in camp I had on wool socks, boots, long underwear, jeans, a wool turtleneck, a down vest, and a nylon windbreaker. Mike emerged from his tent barefooted, in trousers and T-shirt. Nonetheless, he spoke fondly of the arrival of springtime in the north woods, "when you first hear water dripping, see a patch of bare ground, smell mud."

His tiny wife, Kathy, shared a canoe with Ann Mavis, a redhead who had spent much of her free time camping and canoeing in the area. Kathy, in spite of her size, was the hardest worker on the trip. At portages she always made at least two trips, lugging heavy Duluth packs nearly as large as herself.

In the heartland of North American canoeing, the Boundary Waters Canoe Area embraces more than one million acres of protected wilderness in northern Minnesota. Another million acres comprise Quetico Provincial Park, in southern Ontario. Melting glacial ice fed the thousands of lakes and streams that lace this region. For nearly two centuries, rugged voyageurs in birchbark canoes threaded the waterways from Rainy Lake to Grand Portage—a route that now forms the border between the United States and Canada. Late on an Indian summer morning, the author and his group launched their three canoes from the shore of Rainy Lake to paddle and portage through 275 miles of water and woods.

Sam's canoeing partner that first day was John Bartholomew—Bart—who worked for a Minneapolis outfitter and, like Mike, had a background in youth counseling. In fact, as a holdover from his years spent guiding young campers, he could still be awakened in the night by the sound of a tent zipper. Enormously strong, he was a joy to paddle with, though he compulsively sang selections from Broadway hits while paddling. His partner was likely to be treated all day long to tunes from *South Pacific* or *Brigadoon*. He had a good baritone voice but—as with Muzak—it was hard to turn him off.

Sam—absentminded, nearly always late, a pack rat who could hardly bear to leave anything behind—would become a good friend during our travels together. He taught me to look for beauty in unexpected places (a photographer's knack), to relax in the wilderness and savor it, to remain self-possessed in a crisis. He built classically beautiful campfires, painstakingly constructing foundations for them of just the right twigs and branches, feeding them carefully, letting them burn down to golden coals that glowed and flickered and pulsed in the dark breezes.

Our Minnesota trip was the first leg of a journey that would occupy us for a year, and take us and our canoes to varied regions. We sought the waters of canoeists, still and placid lakes, heartstopping streams churned white by rapids, creeks and swamps and rivers that for one reason or another beguile paddlers. We would chase the seasons, turning south for the winter, to the Midwest for spring, then to the canyons of Utah and the streams and lakes of the Rocky Mountains, to the Alaskan wilderness for early autumn.

Our lives would brush those of others across the country. We would learn that an elderly Eskimo lady can serve coffee and doughnuts with the casual grace of an Indiana housewife-conservationist. We would find that while twangs and drawls differ from region to region, people don't. A crusty Yankee storekeeper in Maine would sell us boots—"Just slip into these right quick. Nice fit? Nice?

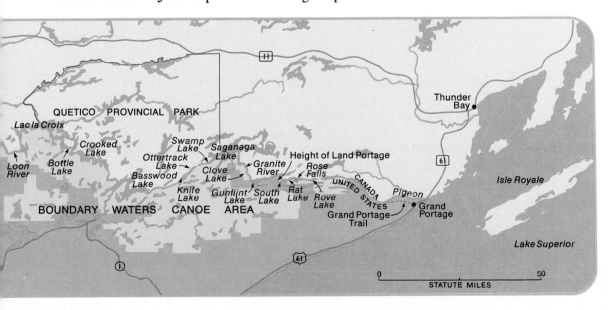

A common loon, piebald in summer plumage, stretches its strong, slender wings. From Minnesota to Maine and beyond, canoeists remember this bird's powerful dives and eerie cry — a sound like wild human laughter.

Nice."—with more enthusiasm but no less success than a moccasin-merchant in Georgia: "Hep y'all?"

Some people we would travel with, and get to know well. Others would figure in brief meetings at gas stations and roadside parks and motels, as boaters caught sight of our canoes, leaned against our fenders, and talked canoeing. "Be sure and do Sugar Creek," said a man in the Ozarks. "Gonna try the Arkansas?" asked another in Oklahoma. A gas-station attendant in Montana wondered, "Whadya call them boats?" He had heard of canoes, it turned out: "Howdya keep 'em from tipping?" I had to admit, "You don't, often." But there wasn't time, then, for stories of rapids and windstorms.

In the afternoon of our second day on Dryweed Island, Indian summer descended around us, and Rainy Lake responded with a smooth sheet of water. Paddling was effortless beneath the cloudless sky, and jackets—and then shirts—came off. Thereafter the golden days fell away like the leaves from an autumn birch—slowly, with grace and elegance. Some days, ranks of fluffy cumulus clouds moved ponderously in from the west. On others, the zinc oxide was passed around to protect noses and foreheads from the sun.

My notebooks reflect pessimism about the weather. For practically every day I find some reference to "ominous clouds" on the horizon, or a "biting wind" that portends winter, or a "dangerous squall" in the distance. But the weather is an important factor during an outing: Wind can stop a canoe in its wake, or swamp it; wetness and cold can quickly turn a trip into drudgery and misery. Yet the beautiful weather held, and all the Minnesotans agreed they had never seen such a fall.

"Watch for high cirrus clouds moving in," Mike told me. "They usually mean a change in weather." Often he proved right, and we had a few days of rain. About ten days out, it sprinkled during the night—enough to move us into tents—and the next day we awoke to a dramatic sky: shafts of sunlight piercing roiling masses of clouds, and some of the blue-gray waves capped with white. The wind whistled through the pine trees, and we paddled that day in ponchos and rain jackets, our hands wet and cold.

As we neared Pater Noster Island in Rainy Lake, a squall appeared on our left, over Canada. Gradually a rainbow materialized, a complete one, both ends visible. A little cloud sprinkled on us, then passed on. The whole episode lasted barely 15 minutes.

A few days later, the wind on Basswood Lake howled into our faces as we worked our way from island to island; it took nearly an hour and a half to make barely two miles. A gale stopped us cold on Clove Lake. We rounded a point into a furious wind, and Sam and I watched as Mike and Ann—paddling as hard as they could—sat perfectly still. Wind-whipped plumes of spray sailed past their heads. We gave up and headed for a nearby campsite.

The wind always bore watching. Bart and I got hung up on a submerged tree one day, and the breeze spun us like a weathervane.

It didn't take me long to appreciate Bart's evaluation of the three things needed for ideal canoeing in Minnesota: "A following wind, a cloudy day, and a strong partner." We changed partners every day, both to facilitate getting acquainted and to maintain compatibility. Each morning we checked Bart's elaborate chart to see who our day's partner would be. It was complicated by the fact that neither Bart nor Mike would condescend to paddle in the bow.

I learned there is something to be said for both the stern and the bow: The bow requires little attention, so your mind can wander at will and concentrate on important things—like clouds and birds and reflections on the water. But it's uncomfortable and can be boring. The alternative is more comfortable and more interesting, since steering is the responsibility of the sternperson (a liberated and widely accepted term we first heard at a canoe clinic in the hills of North Carolina). But paddling in the stern demands your attention all day. Often, we changed positions at noon.

Floating rest stops came every couple of hours. We would maneuver the canoes alongside one another and loll back beneath the cloudless skies, with maybe a faint breeze blowing and a loon or two calling in the distance. It was a good time for passing around candy bars, checking maps, discussing mileages and campsites.

We were retracing a part of the 18th-century route of the voyageurs, French Canadians who canoed into the interior wilderness with trade goods, and home again to Montreal with furs. Their birchbark canoes could carry 3,000 pounds of cargo and six men. They were small men—so as not to take up precious freight space—but incredibly tough. At portages, they commonly carried two 90-pound packs—and jogged doing it! If it rained they paddled naked, to keep their clothes dry. As might be expected, they were boastful men. It was said that they could "live hard, lie hard, sleep hard, eat dogs." It was also said that "Voyageurs never see little wolves."

As my hands hardened, my arm and shoulder muscles developed, and my nose lost its first layer of sunburn, I learned to enjoy canoeing, and the days passed quickly. Pale green boulders might rise silently from the depths to pass beneath us. One day on Lac la Croix we crossed a shallow spot, and beneath us grew a miniature forest—ferns and tall tree-like water plants standing perfectly still. Hundreds of silver minnows flitted among them like birds.

A blessed day came when a stiff breeze blew from behind us. We rollicked along before it, roller-coastering up and down the waves at the unheard-of canoe speed of five or six miles an hour.

Not all days passed so pleasantly. Often our feet were wet from morning till evening; portages nearly always involved wading as we loaded and unloaded the canoes a few feet from the rocky shores.

One rainy evening, darkness caught us on Rove Lake. With the stars and moon obscured by clouds, I could barely see Sam in the bow. We paddled cautiously down the long, narrow lake straining to see. The lapping and splash of the water against the shore became ominous in the blackness. When Bart and Ann got hung up on a submerged log, we called it a night and retreated to a nearby portage and camped on the beach. Our fire that night, when we got it going, outdid them all in cheeriness and comfort.

Weariness overcame us at times. Gunflint Lake, seven miles long, seemed endless. With our destination always in sight and seemingly never any nearer, I developed a taste for smaller lakes and streams that would last throughout the coming year. The miles pass quicker in small waters.

But on long lakes you sometimes get an entrancing view of a canoe: In the distance, its wet paddles flash synchronously in the sun like gills, and it looks like a living creature approaching.

The lakes varied in size from Rainy—35 miles long—to Rat Lake, shallow and muddy and barely 300 yards across.

"The voyageurs were afraid of Rat Lake," Mike told me. "They thought that the mud had no bottom, that they might be sucked down into the muck." Indeed, even at the edge I couldn't reach a firm bottom with my paddle.

Swamp Lake was ugly, shallow, full of weeds, and its shore had been blackened by a recent fire—but it was on Swamp that I heard the only frogs of the trip: a low guttural rumble.

The rivers, shallow and slow in autumn, had no rapids to speak of. The Granite offered some excitement, though. Going upstream, we had to pull the canoes through the riffles. Wading in the icy water over mossy submerged rocks is fun until you slip in up to your waist. Mike and Ann barely avoided serious trouble when Ann, leading the way and towing the canoe, stepped in a hole and lost her grip on the bowline. The canoes, heavily loaded, seemed to have minds of their own as they fought to get away from us.

Canoeing is one thing, but portaging is another. And in Minnesota's lakes it seems you can't have one without the other, for usually

On snarling rivers and arduous portage trails, hardy French-Canadian voyageurs blazed canoe routes deep into North America's unmapped interior, opening the Indians' Northwest to the colonial fur trade.

the only way to get from one lake to the other is up and over. Our first portage, from Rainy to Namakan Lake, was an 80-rod trek. (The rod, an old English unit of measure, is standard for describing portages—perhaps because "80 rods" sounds easier than 440 yards.) Scarlet maple leaves, wet with dew, blanketed the path and cast a rosy light over us; it was like hiking through cotton candy.

But many portages were dreaded. Huffing through the woods—often on a steep, slippery path—with an 85-pound canoe resting on my shoulders made me feel like the business end of a pile driver, being hammered deeper into the ground at every step. Our Duluth packs weighed 40 or 50 pounds apiece. They're fitted with tumplines that fit across the forehead, supposedly to distribute some of the weight onto your neck. The only time I tried using a tumpline I danced backward, my arms flailing, and nearly fell down.

Bart did a similar dance one day at an extremely muddy portage. After gallantly offering Ann a piggyback ride through the muck, he got his feet stuck in the goo, lost his balance, staggered as she jumped free, and sat down hard on the only rock at the portage.

At Height of Land Portage, where water flows north to Hudson Bay, east to the Atlantic, and south to the Gulf of Mexico, we participated in a ceremony that parodied one the voyageurs held when they reached this spot. Sam and I danced around a boulder singing "Yankee Doodle" and "God Save the Queen," while Bart and Mike sprinkled us with cedar branches dipped in water. After this initiation, we're honor bound never to kiss a voyageur's wife without her permission.

Because of the lateness of the season, we had the rivers and lakes practically to ourselves. We saw a few fishermen here and there, three or four canoes, a houseboat on Rainy Lake, but mostly we traveled through solitude. On the Pigeon River a helicopter appeared, evidently spotted us, and hovered low overhead for a few moments. We couldn't identify it, and it alarmed everyone at first — some emergency at home? — but soon went on its way.

More than two weeks out, we stopped at Gunflint Lodge. It was odd, approaching over the still lake, once again to hear cars running, screen doors slamming, human voices. We depleted the candy-bar supply and looked at ourselves — appalled — in a mirror. The managers took us in stride, partly because they were accustomed to grubby campers, partly because they were in-laws of Kathy's and had been expecting us. While they enjoyed a brief reunion, the rest of us prepared to press on to a choice campsite. That was the only time we were indoors in the BWCA.

Finding a good campsite — a spot easily accessible, with a fire ring, tent sites, plenty of firewood, and a pleasant view — became something we all looked forward to. As soon as the canoes hit the beach — usually around four or five o'clock — the scramble began, as people laid claim to flat and comfortable tent sites, began gathering firewood, and changed into dry clothes.

The voyageurs had a similar routine. One of them addressed a group of Oberlin College students in 1843: "We now gather before a cheerful fire, pull off our leggins and moccasons, and hang them by the fire to dry, putting on dry socks and moccasons. The cook urges forward the supper. . . ."

Kathy usually took the lead in preparing our supper. She often made bannock, a delicious and adaptable bread the voyageurs ate, and here's her recipe: "2 cups white flour. 2 cups cornmeal and/or whole wheat flour. 2 small spoons baking powder. Some salt.

"Mix this up and add 2 large spoons oil plus any other flavorings: cinnamon, honey, peanut butter, raisins, dried fruit. Work in about a cup and a half of water till all the dough comes together in a ball. Press dough into a greased fry pan — a cast iron skillet is excellent (also heavy).

"Have a friend chop some good firewood and cook bannock over hot coals for about 20-30 minutes. (Underneath side should be brown.) Flip and cook some more and enjoy the fire for another 15-20 mins. When you think bannock is done leave on fire another 10 mins. to be sure.

"Best eaten with lots of butter and shared with a squirrel or two, Canada jays, and a friend."

"The old-timers used to make it right in their 50-pound sacks of flour," Kathy told me. "They'd just keep kneading until it wouldn't absorb any more flour."

Rules of BWCA prohibit use of foods in bottles or tin cans, so we ate mostly the freeze-dried dinners developed in the past few years primarily for backpackers. The franks and beans were a big hit. For lunch the menu included peanut butter, jelly, rye crackers (six apiece), bannock, salami, cheese, lemonade, and chocolate bars.

I had hoped to have fish for supper at least every other night, but as it turned out, in three weeks on the water, I caught exactly one fish — a pitiful bass that at least provided everyone with a morsel. I consoled myself with thoughts of all the other fishing waters we would be canoeing. Probably I'll be sick of fish by the time the year is over, I thought.

Campsites often took on the look of a settlement of squatters, with clotheslines rigged for wet clothes, sleeping bags opened and flung across bushes to air, and clutter from emptied packs scattered. Familiar sounds quickly made a new site seem like home: the steady *chunk chunk chunk* of Mike's ax as he and Bart split wood, waves washing the beach, maybe a grouse or two making a rackety take-off in the underbrush, chickadees jabbering in the trees.

Campsites meant strolls through the tall, still pine trees, the scent of balsam luring us on like a perfume. We might come across a grouse, or squirrels, or some deer sign — or a dead bird, everything gone but the tiny, miraculous bones, dazzlingly white against the somber forest floor. Then, snug in our tents, we would listen to the wind snapping the tent flaps, twigs and grit plunking against the canvas, and feel safe and secure.

There came a day — nearly three weeks out — when the weather changed from autumn to winter. A strong, blustery, confused wind sent yellow birch leaves whirling far out across the water. Most of the trees near the shore were blown bare, but patches of yellow, farther inland, marked trees out of the wind.

The birds and beasts of the Minnesota lake country add charm to an already splendid landscape. On a hike one day above Rose Falls, a gentle cascade that tumbles into Rose Lake, I came to a narrow plank bridge. It was mostly in shade, but in a splash of sunshine, just on the downstream edge, sat a chipmunk on its hind legs. It rested in the sun gazing at the waterfall as it methodically peeled a pine cone. I couldn't help thinking it had picked the sunny, scenic spot just for a picnic. When it saw me, it squeaked like a child's rubber squeeze toy and skittered into the brush.

While camped on Dryweed Island, we could hear beavers working in the night. They lived across a small inlet, and the sound of their munching carried clearly in the still evening air. Occasionally one would dive — with a "plunk" — or slap its tail against the water with a sharp crack. In the morning, fresh-cut branches floated near the shore, green leaves still attached.

The next evening we went down to the shore to try to get a look at the animals. We stood in the gathering darkness, then held our breath as a V appeared in the water off to the right.

"Mink," whispered Kathy.

It glided silently ashore on the opposite bank near the beaver lodge; through the gloom it was barely visible, a shadow a little darker than the night. Then it was in the water again, diving.

"It's fishing," said Kathy. Sure enough, *(Continued on page 30)*

*F*aced with a choice of channels, chief guide Mike Lande checks his map for a safe route as wind gusts and granite clouds signal a squall. While paddling to maintain speed and steering toward a passage, he scans the border of Crooked Lake for landmarks apparent to the

expert. In the Boundary Waters, few vantage points exist—canoeists must learn to "read the shoreline." Navigators come to discern subtle differences in shading and depth along the fringe of a lake, spotting narrows and bays where the untrained eye sees a continuous shore.

Quaking aspens spire above their reflections as a gauze of morning mist brushes the surface of Ottertrack Lake. Dense forests of balsam, spruce, and pine mantle the Boundary Waters region, sheltering a rich and varied fauna. Black bear, deer, moose, and the endangered timber wolf roam these woodlands, while game fish — walleye, lake trout, and northern pike — lure anglers through the mazy channels. Cold, sweet, and pure, lake waters refresh thirsty

20

canoeists. *Above, Mike Lande demonstrates "paddle-drinking," a technique attributed to the voyageurs. Droplets spatter as he plunges his paddle into the lake; a split second later, it pops up like a cork into his hands. Quickly, he raises the blade so the water that rolls down the edge will flow into his mouth. "It's fast and efficient, and you get a good big drink," explains Sam Abell, "but only Mike could do it well. The rest of us just dribbled down our chins."*

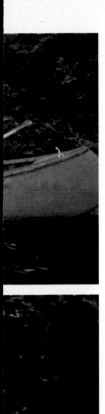

Shortcut that led to a crisis: To avoid a cumbersome portage, Mike Lande and Ann Mavis decided to tow their canoe through a chute on the Granite River. After aligning the boat with the bank, Ann grasped the bowline while Mike steadied the stern. Plodding against the current, they edged carefully over the smooth rocks studding the streambed. Suddenly, Ann slipped into a hole, waist-deep in the cold, swift water. As the rope slid through her fingers, the current swept the bow away from the shore, leaving the craft broadside in the channel. In this dangerous position, the canoe could tip, fill with water, and flip its contents into the rapids. At top, Ann strains to keep her balance while Mike grips the gunwale and reaches for the bowline. Snatching it, he yanked the slack cord and tugged the bow toward the bank. At center, Mike holds the line taut, striding closer to the bank; Ann struggles to regain her footing in the racing water. Finally, she scrambled to the shore to take over the bowline. At bottom, Mike points to the hazardous area, shouting a warning to the next team of paddlers. With their canoe once again in proper position—parallel with the current—Ann pulls the rope to go on upstream. As veterans caution, when in doubt, avoid the rapids; no canoe ever swamped on a portage.

Windbound and stuck-in-the-mud: A quiet cove shelters Ann from a howling gale at Clove Lake that stalled the canoeists on rough waters. "We rounded a point into a furious wind, and Sam and I watched as Mike and Ann—paddling as hard as they could—sat perfectly still," recalls Ron. "We gave it up for the day and headed for a nearby campsite." Another obstacle challenged the team on portage trails: mud. At the end of a portage between Lac la Croix and Bottle Lake, John Bartholomew—Bart—gallantly offered to carry Ann on his back across the mud. Trudging through the deep goo, Bart teetered and lost his balance. Ann jumped off and Bart fell, sitting, onto a rock. Weak with laughter, Ann bends to lift him from the gluey mire.

*S*till waters ripple gently as Mike and Kathy Lande paddle across South Lake toward their evening campsite. Late-afternoon sunlight gilds the fall foliage on the hills. Although about 170,000 visitors explore the Boundary Waters each year, the author's group spotted few people on their three-week journey. "Mostly we canoed

through solitude," recalls Ron. Almost daily, migrating birds glided overhead. Honking loudly, a wedge of Canada geese flaps southward. At left, flames warm the camp coffeepot; rocks rimming the grate help retain the heat from the coals.

*F*riendly words and an offering of bannock coax a Canada jay to perch on Kathy's outstretched fingers. Called "whiskey jacks" or "camp robbers," these inquisitive birds frequent campsites for handouts — or a chance to snitch a meal. "We almost always had a couple of them begging nearby," says Ron. "One landed on the edge of the bannock pan while the bread was cooking and nearly set its tail on fire." At left, a ruffed grouse strolls through shaded grass along a portage trail. A medley of birds — bald eagles and white-throated sparrows, ducks and owls and ospreys, hawks and chickadees — nests in the Boundary Waters wilderness.

every time it surfaced it had something in its mouth — small fish, I suppose. It repeated the maneuver three times, then moved away into the darkness.

About a week later we met a beaver swimming toward us. Preoccupied with its own affairs, it passed us just ten yards away without so much as a glance. Similarly, a young mink ran beside us with a curious humpbacked lope along the grassy shore of the Pigeon River for a few minutes. Our canoes made no sound at all as we glided along, so perhaps it didn't see us.

One breezy day Bart told me a chipmunk story: "It was a day a lot like this one. There was quite a wind blowing, rollers a couple of feet high. We were canoeing down a lake north of here when one of the guys noticed a chipmunk in the water. It was headed for a shore a good six miles away; obviously it wouldn't make it. We tried to catch it, but it panicked and swam in circles. We tried and tried till we about wore it out. Finally we used the canoes to herd it onto the nearest shore. It jumped on a log and chattered at us — mad. You know, nothing sounds madder than a ticked-off chipmunk."

Birds were on the move throughout the trip. Ducks and geese, headed south, passed over us nearly every day. On Basswood Lake, a flock of geese came low overhead, saw us, and — amid furious honking — let their careful formation disintegrate into chaos. They soon re-formed and headed east, then turned south once more.

At night owls hooted their melancholy songs across the waters like little verbal gifts, and once I was awakened, near dawn, by the sound of wings rushing past the tent. Probably an owl. Or perhaps a goldeneye duck, whose specific name — *clangula* — means "a little noise," befitting the sound of its wings in flight.

At night, too, the loons chortled madly to one another. It's a demented but lovely sound, almost impossible to describe, part yodel, part sob. On Basswood Lake one nearby called to one far away for half an hour. Another, on Crooked Lake, spent about the same amount of time calling and answering its own echo.

We often saw the big wary birds swimming. On Knife Lake a flock of ten or eleven swam majestically before us, barking like puppies — hooty, high-pitched sounds. They would peer down into the depths like snorkelers, wiggle their tail feathers, then dive. Alarmed by us, they began diving more frequently and swimming farther — perhaps 50 yards — before surfacing. We herded them like sheep, or they lured us on, for an hour. "In the air they look tail-heavy," said Kathy, "as if their wings had been placed too far back."

Early in the trip we had come across a bald eagle perched on the top of a dead pine tree. As we moved closer it spread its wings and hopped — like someone going off a diving board — into the air. It circled us once, then headed for the horizon. We saw several after that, soaring, rising in spirals on the thermals. We watched one for five minutes and never saw it flap its wings.

Canada jays, also called whiskey jacks, moved into our campsites almost as quickly as we did. Gray birds with black BB eyes, they are amazingly tame. We almost always had a couple of them begging nearby. One landed on the edge of the bannock pan while the bread was cooking and nearly set its tail on fire. Another came to rest on the wet and slippery prow of an upside-down canoe. Wings outstretched for balance, that bird skied down the slope like a kid on a skateboard.

Cree Indians called the smoke-colored bird *wiiskachaan*. That evolved into whiskey jack, a good name. In the 1780's, David Thompson, an employee of the Hudson's Bay Company, described the bird: "easily taken by a snare, and brought into the room, seems directly quite at home; when spirits is offered, it directly drinks, is soon drunk and fastens itself anywhere till sober."

For twenty minutes one day we inadvertently pursued a little mallard down the Loon River. It would let us come just so close, then take off and fly a couple of hundred yards downstream, then wait until we caught up, then take off again. At last it turned in the water to face us, bobbing like a decoy. I could almost see it screwing up the courage to deal with us once and for all. Finally, with a resolute quack, it raced down the narrow river straight toward us, wings and feet thrashing madly. We all held our breath as it passed low overhead, its little black legs still running. "Get your feet up!" yelled Bart, and up they went.

Of all the wonders in Minnesota, the most wondrous were the nighttime skies. One memorable night we could see not only the Milky Way, nearly solid with stars, but also its reflection in the lake— beauty tossed back and forth across an immeasurable gulf at unthinkable speed. Another night we sat late on a rocky peninsula with honey in our tea and peace in our hearts, and watched a cosmic display—Venus, doubled by its reflections; shooting stars; the Milky Way sprawled above us; and the northern lights flickering on the horizon—as our little promontory wheeled toward the dawn.

Wriggling north from placid lakes, the 92-mile Allagash Wilderness Waterway twists through 300,000 acres of Maine's dense woodlands.

Minnesota skies stretched broad and blue over us until we left the state, to drive north of Lake Superior toward Maine. We had parted from our new friends with regret. They represent the new wilderness ethic, we concluded, city people who come to the woods to replenish their lives. Now we wanted to find Leonard Pelletier at his home in St. Francis, Maine, just across the border from Canada. He, as we had heard, represents an older experience of the wilds.

Leonard grew up in Allagash, Maine, about the time of World War I. His father operated a ferry across the Allagash River, and

Leonard recalls being called from school to man the windlass that propelled it. He dropped out of school after the eighth grade, and is sorry; he would have liked to play football.

"Sundays were our fun," he says. "In the spring, when the logs were running, we'd ride them from my grandfather's house around a horseshoe in the river, then walk back and get on another one."

As a young man Leonard worked as a logger, into the woods in August and home the following spring. He ate beans and molasses all winter. "We were cold and wet every day. There were no chain saws or skidders — we used handsaws and axes and horses." In the spring, they coaxed the reluctant logs down the icy Allagash.

In his 20's, Leonard went to work for the Maine Fish and Game Department as a game warden. He lived alone in a little cabin on Eagle Lake and did most of his work at night, trailing and apprehending poachers. Often he was out all night, with nothing but his snowshoes and pack. He slept on beds of fir boughs. In one 24-hour period, he snowshoed 43 miles through the awesome silences of the north woods.

Once, out of uniform, he dropped in on a young couple who didn't know him — "hard working, good people." The man had a job chopping wood for 75 cents a cord. "For supper they gave me fresh deer liver — obviously poached, since it wasn't deer season. I ate it. It was delicious. I couldn't bring myself to arrest that man."

Marriage and a family brought the need for more money, so Leonard returned to logging for a few years, but he finally opted for happiness and freedom, gave up logging for good, and returned to the Fish and Game job. He was a warden with them for 31 years, and today three of his four sons and one brother are wardens.

He can speak fluent French, imitate a loon or Carol Burnett, start a fire in snow with one match after two days of rain, stand up and pole a loaded canoe through rapids, upstream or down. He can patch a gashed canoe with spruce pitch and strips of handkerchief, and produce pancakes as light as a whitecap. He calls the twigs and leaves that rattle down onto a tent at night "dry spills," and his red stocking cap a "bonnet." "I saw the last of the best of this country," Leonard says, and he probably did. Happily for us, he agreed to accompany Sam and me on a 92-mile canoe trip down the Allagash Wilderness Waterway, a protected chain of lakes and rivers.

Leonard has spent a lifetime in canoes — can build them, widen them, or lengthen them — but is mystified by the popularity of the sport of canoeing. "I don't see how anybody could get a thrill out of riding down the Allagash in a canoe," he says. While he was growing up, canoeing was not a form of recreation; it was simply the most practical way of getting around on the rivers and lakes of Maine. Familiarity has bred, if not contempt, at least indifference.

Leonard's philosophy of canoeing and camping was markedly different from Mike's and Bart's: "Take everything you might need." A motor, gas cans, a saw, a gun, a chair — all got packed in his canoe. "Be as comfortable as you can." If it's cold, find a cabin, or build a lean-to, or saw down a dead tree and make a bonfire three feet high.

So we were ready for anything when we set off late one afternoon from the shore of Telos Lake. It's the most popular put-in for canoe parties on the Allagash, and popular is hardly the word for it. In 1962, about 1,000 people traveled down the river; in the three summer months of 1975, about 7,000. During a fine week in August you might find 700 people—a regular flotilla of canoes. November turned out to be a good time for our trip.

It felt marvelous to be back in our canoe again, after the long drive from Minnesota. Chamberlain Lake lay placid before us, its rocky shores lined with spruce and pines, Mount Katahdin and its sister peaks looming behind us.

Canoeing turned out to be much the same as in Minnesota. The lakes are much smaller, as narrow as rivers in many places, and connected by necks called thoroughfares. There are few portages, though below Lock Dam we had to drag the canoes for half a mile down a two-foot-wide trickle.

Lakes comprise the first third of the Allagash; then the river takes over, with a nice current to carry you along. The only troublesome area is the nine-mile stretch of Chase Rapids, also called Chase's Carry—a reference to an agreement with the rangers who, for a fee, will carry your cargo around the rapids in a truck.

The water was very low the day we tackled Chase's Carry, and its speed and shallowness caused Sam and me a good deal of trouble. Rushing along, shouting directions to each other over the roar of the water, we dodged boulder after boulder. Sideways in a strong current a canoe is in a hazardous position, so with each boulder—or whenever we ran aground—out we would hop, tow the canoe to a likely-looking channel, and clamber back in. But the rocks and hazards came too fast; there was no time between crises. Leonard, ahead of us, stood in his canoe, carefully picking his way through, his steel-tipped pole dragging along the bottom with a sound like billiard balls banging into one another. His method was obviously best. Standing, he could see farther and pick the best route. With his pole he could vary his speed, slow down, even stop. He let the current do all the work. Sam and I got very, very wet.

Later Leonard told us of a young couple he had seen come through Chase's Carry a couple of years earlier. They were soaked, disgruntled and unhappy, their gear all lost, their "little light canoe" damaged. Leonard said to the woman, "Next year when you come back, I expect you'll have a better canoe." "I'll have a better man, too," she snapped.

As in Minnesota, we had a spooky experience in the dark, this time on Eagle Lake. Leonard had gone on ahead to our campsite, but Sam and I had five or six miles yet to go as darkness began to fall. The shorelines lost their detail; the moon appeared over one shoulder and Venus over the other. Thunder rumbled in the distance; a flash of lightning illuminated the lake. Rollers rushed beneath us, and it was pitch dark when we finally rounded a point and saw the lighted cabin where Leonard awaited us. It was good to be inside that night, to hear the rain on the roof and the embers crackling in the stove.

Though we seldom saw other people, we knew they were all around us. Jet bombers and fighters from an Air Force base often flashed low overhead, their thunder making the very trees quake. Near Thoroughfare Brook we passed under a bridge just as an enormous truck, piled high with logs, rumbled overhead. Logging is permitted to within 400 to 800 feet of the water's edge, and a day seldom passed when we couldn't hear chain saws and skidders.

"The original proposal called for a park three times the size of the present one," Leonard told us. "The logging companies bitterly opposed *any* park. When they lost the fight, they changed their position and now point to the Allagash as an example of their concern for the environment. They're proud of it. They make it seem like it was their idea."

Paul McCann, manager of public affairs for the Great Northern Paper Company, says that while the paper companies didn't particularly want such a park, they did not oppose the state legislation that created it. "I think they realized it was the best deal they could get," he told me. "There were some big guns favoring it— Senator Ed Muskie and Secretary of the Interior Stewart Udall, for instance—and the landowners realized there was going to be a park established, either by the state, where they could maintain some control, or by the federal government.

"Frankly, many of the foresters of the paper companies feel that the Waterway area was managed better when it was privately owned. Now it's badly overused, they feel. They say they were applying special management considerations to the Waterway long before Udall and Muskie urged its preservation.

"Naturally, any regulation is an added expense. That's a fact of life. And nobody in the industry likes to take land out of multiple use and dedicate it entirely to a single purpose. But there's also a realization among management here that there is a place and a need for some wilderness areas."

Relics of early logging days can be found scattered along the Allagash. On the shore of Chamberlain Lake an old paddle-wheeler, once used to tow log booms, lies disintegrating, its deck planks scarred by thousands of tiny holes from the loggers' hobnailed boots. Just back from the shore of Eagle Lake, alone in the forest, two massive and silent locomotives sit abandoned and rusting on tracks that go nowhere. They've been there since the Great Depression. Rows of pulp cars—like cattle cars with wooden slat sides— sit rotting in the brush, their sides collapsed and moss-covered, young trees growing up through them.

Our old friends the Canada jays—called "gorbies" by Leonard —performed the same tricks for us they had in Minnesota. "Old-timers believe they're departed woodsmen, come back for a hand-out," he told us. Ducks, frantic to get aloft, raced before us down the lakes, wings slapping the water with a sound like typewriter keys.

Leonard spoke with wonder and pity of the animals' ability to make it through the harsh Maine winters, of ducks that stay, standing on the ice on their "little thin legs." A mouse I saw had solved the problem by moving into the Churchill Dam ranger cabin. It was the fattest mouse I ever saw, almost perfectly round.

Once again we had miraculous weather. Northern Maine in November can be bitter, but though it was often cold, the blizzards held off. Our first morning out, I awoke in the tent with the hot sun shining in my eyes. By the time I was up and dressed a mist was falling. Before breakfast was over it had turned into a shower, then snow flurries. By noon it was clear again.

Snow fell on us all day as we approached Round Pond. The wind, mostly at our backs, would swing around suddenly and splatter our faces with cold flakes, or send them flying along beside us, parallel to the river. The bottom four inches of my jeans were frozen solid when we got to camp. The next morning we paddled through sheets of ice that tinkled and shattered like breaking glass.

At Round Pond we stayed in a warden's cabin Leonard had built 30 years before. "It's small," he said, "but that's what a warden wants. You can heat it in no time, even when it's 40 below."

Approaching Allagash Falls, we came upon a sign: "DANGEROUS FALLS — ALL PARTIES CARRY." Dangerous indeed! The river tumbles and roars over tiers of rocks, falling 35 feet. We portaged about an eighth of a mile. For miles downstream clumps of white froth floated on the river. "Frothbergs," Sam called them.

We ended our trip late one evening, the lights of the little town of Allagash winking a welcome. Oddly, as we stood by the river in the dark, its laughing ripples sounding cold and lonesome, a total eclipse of the moon occurred. We watched as the earth's shadow crept across its face, finally leaving nothing but a pale golden outline. As the moon winked out, the stars winked on. It was as though someone had pushed an old-fashioned light switch: Push the top button, the bottom one pops out. Stars appeared in their billions. In the chilly night air my breath condensed — a puff of silver dew — and rose toward them.

Enough of this cold! Sam and I agreed, so we lashed the canoes onto our van and — like the ducks — headed South.

"It was the fattest mouse I ever saw, almost perfectly round," says Ron, describing a chubby rodent that spent the winter snug in an Allagash ranger's cabin.

Wilderness playground, woodland sanctuary: Running northward through Maine's rich timberlands, the Allagash Wilderness Waterway draws thousands of sportsmen to its forests, lakes, and streams each year. Spruce and fir trees blanket the shores of Chamberlain Lake (lower left), once the scene of massive log drives. Preserved as a part of the National Wild and Scenic Rivers System, the Allagash now carries canoes—not logs—along its winding route. A fringe of uncut forest, 400 to 800 feet wide, borders the Waterway; beyond that zone, selective timber harvesting continues. Below, a truck laden with logs rumbles across Churchill Dam. Most canoeists drive to Telos Lake, the Waterway's southern terminus, to begin their journey; a few choose to fly (far left). For the first 34 miles of the watercourse, paddlers skim across serene lakes and ponds. Then, below Churchill Dam, the river brawls. For nine rollicking miles, canoes buck and slap through Chase Rapids—the white-water stretch of the Allagash. At left, Bert Drake paddles the choppy chute, while his son, Pete, grins with fear and excitement.

Like a white-water gondolier, guide Leonard Pelletier poles his canoe through shallow rapids below Long Lake Dam. Knees flexed for jolts, he studies the foaming waves ahead to select the safest course. In rocky passages, experienced Maine canoeists like Leonard often switch from paddle to pole, a holdover from the earlier days of the flat-bottomed logging boats. Along the opposite shore, the remains of an old log-boom pier — used to funnel floating timber through the dam — jut from the bank. Above, russet weeds surround an abandoned barn at Chamberlain Farm. A popular lunch stop for paddlers, the 600-acre clearing borders Chamberlain Lake — once the headquarters for the region's lumbering operations. During the 1800's, farmers cultivated Chamberlain's hayfields to feed draft horses that hauled towboats heavy with food and supplies along the waterway.

Morning snow flurries swirl above Round Pond as Leonard pokes his setting pole against the rocky bank to test its new point. A former logger and game warden, Leonard has paddled and poled the Allagash waters for more than half a century. Now retired, he builds

and repairs boats, and occasionally guides canoeists. A lively storyteller and resourceful riverman, he can "imitate a loon or Carol Burnett . . . patch a gashed canoe with spruce pitch and strips of handkerchief, and produce pancakes as light as a whitecap," says Ron.

2

The Swamp and the Suwannee

I LOVE THE SOUTH, and I love its people. As in my home region, the Midwest, folks in the South are folksy. I love their friendliness and openness and the way they sort their priorities: In a supermarket at Waycross, Georgia, an entire aisle was labeled "Assorted Moon Pies." A sign outside Gibson's, a discount department store, noted the week's specials: "Trolling Motor, $79.95; Mayonnaise, 67¢." And a sign in front of a dry cleaner's advised, "To cleanse the stains of sin, wash in the blood of Jesus."

I love the way Southerners talk. When we left a barefoot young man who had helped us transport our gear, I said, "So long, take care of yourself." "Y'all take care of y'alls' selves," he answered. It was a long way—about 1,400 miles—from Leonard's Yankee twang.

The robins, moving down from the North, had arrived in Georgia before us. Roads and highways were alive with thousands of them, pecking single-mindedly in the grassy shoulders. Beyond them, pine-tree plantations stretched for miles; paper companies here harvest pine trees the way Iowa farmers harvest corn.

Like the robins, we had come for the winter—to canoe in the Okefenokee Swamp and down the Suwannee River. A Geographic colleague, researcher Toni Eugene, joined Sam and me for the swamp stint, after collecting basic facts for us. The Okefenokee, more than 640 square miles of moody cypress trees, sedge "prairies," sandy islands, and lakes, mostly belongs to the Okefenokee National Wildlife Refuge. It is managed by the Fish and Wildlife Service of the Department of the Interior. Refuge personnel have charted color-coded canoe trails through the swamp, marked them, maintained them, and built shelters along them for overnight stays.

Sun-flecked waters of the Okefenokee Swamp create a starry field for a white water lily. The setting took shape between 500,000 and 1,250,000 years ago when the Atlantic extended inland about 75 miles west of the present coastline. Then changes in ocean and continental margin left a basin that eventually became the swamp.

When we arrived at Kingfisher Landing—one of three put-in points for canoeists—the morning was obscured by a heavy fog. Above it, Spanish moss swayed in the breeze like seaweed in a gentle current. I suspect that Sam felt a hint of apprehension, as I did. Our knowledge of swamps came from movies and books; a swamp would be a muggy and dark place, alive with malaria and menace. Toni had never been in a swamp either. Her canoeing experience was limited to the Brandywine Creek near her Pennsylvania home, and vacations on Georgian Bay in Canada. Good-natured and imperturbable, she helped us load the canoes to the gunwales with food and cargo—including a gas stove and lantern. In addition, she had diverting mini-lectures ready.

"Did you know," she would say, "that Okefenokee has been spelled at least 77 different ways over the years, by people trying to reproduce the Indian sounds? One of its first appearances on a map was in 1769, when it was spelled Ekanphaenoka." Other efforts included Owaquephenogaw and Ouakaphanoke. Originally, *o-kee* meant "water," *ee-ka-na* meant "earth," and *fe-no-kee* meant "trembling." In fact, there are places where vegetation has taken root on semi-floating masses of muck. Stepped upon, the land undulates in visible waves, making the very trees and bushes sway.

As the mist burned away and the sun warmed us, the swamp seemed less ominous. Paddling wasn't difficult. Current exists, but as a slow sliding of the waters southward. The Okefenokee is a collecting basin serving as a pool for the slightly higher area to the west and the northwest. Its general elevation is 125 feet above sea level, but within 15 miles to the east of the swamp the elevation rises to 163 feet, blocking drainage in that direction. Both the Suwannee and the St. Marys Rivers are born here, the first to run southwestward to the Gulf of Mexico, the second to reach the Atlantic just above Jacksonville.

Though we paddled slowly, the hours passed quickly. The so-called prairies, broad meadowlike areas of sedge and lily pads, smelled dry and dusty, like a summer wheat field. I preferred them to the more jungly stretches; the canoeing was easy, except when the wind nudged the canoes into the lily pads. Still, sitting in a canoe, I sometimes felt hemmed in by the nodding sedge. A scenic overlook would have been appreciated, and six feet would do.

We found the trails carefully marked. Little white-tipped posts appear at regular intervals and wherever you might make a wrong turn. At every mile is a signboard in the color of your trail (red or green, for instance) to give the mileage from your put-in point. Other signs identify lakes or points of interest.

Dazzling white herons and egrets stood and watched us pass, honking and hooting occasionally in alarm. Turkey buzzards, circling overhead, sent their shadows flitting across the canoes. High above them, jets murmured across the blue sky, leaving their white trails. For long periods we talked not at all, silenced by the warm sun and the hush of the swamp.

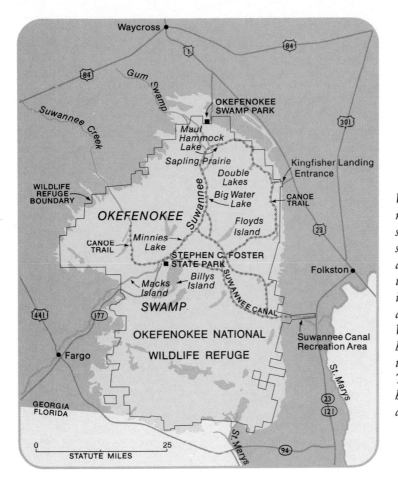

About noon we paused for a floating lunch. Scrambling back and forth across the packed cargo called for dexterity and a steady nerve. Conversation was businesslike: "Can you reach the peanut butter?" "I'll steady the canoe—you find the apples." After lunch we leaned back across the packs and dozed for a while, the sun hot and dry in our nostrils.

Paradoxically, the wetness of the swamp turned out to be an illusion. In winter, though there is water everywhere, the plants are tinder-dry, and fire periodically sweeps through them.

As the lazy afternoon wore on, we misjudged our mileage. About the time we expected to reach our first campsite, we came to Double Lakes—not halfway. We bestirred ourselves and paddled hard, but darkness caught us with miles still to go. The sun set gloriously before us, and the Spanish moss seemed to drip redness. The moon came up behind us, blinking in and out of scudding clouds. Sam and Toni, in the other canoe, gradually pulled ahead of me, and before I was quite ready I found myself alone in the dark.

The swamp came to life around me with grunts and croaks, hoots and splashes. Patches of brightness and darkness cast me one minute in velvety blackness, the next in a luminous clarity. I soon convinced myself that I was hopelessly lost, but I kept going, peering anxiously into the night to see the little white-tipped posts.

After about an hour I stopped paddling, sat very still, and called: "Sa-a-a-m!" No answer. Something rustled in the dry leaves beside me and I called again, louder. An answer, nearer than expected. They were just half a mile or so ahead. I hurried on and found them resting their paddles in a pool of moonlight. Within ten minutes we saw a sign for the shelter, and soon its slanted roof.

These shelters, erected where no solid land is available for camping, are simple 20-by-28-foot structures, something like an old-fashioned wooden pavilion at a picnic ground. They usually have a little pier, and a chemical toilet.

Shaky knees—partly from sitting so long, partly from nerves— afflicted us as we unloaded and set up the stove and lantern and put the soup on.

"We'd have been all right, even if we got lost," Sam remarked. "We couldn't have strayed very far from the trail, and the chance of anything harming us is pretty remote."

"How about snakes?" I said. "Or alligators?"

"They wouldn't hurt you if you just stayed in the canoe."

After supper we talked for a while, but we were tired after a long day and turned in early.

Cypress knees, gnarled growths from tree roots, rise in the swamp's waters. Mystery surrounds the forms, which reach as high as five feet. Botanists do not know their function — or if they have one.

It was chilly that first night; too cool for bugs, I thought, but mosquitoes buzzed in and out of our ears. I awoke once in bright moonlight, with hard shadows patterning the sleeping bats, and listened to the screams and splashes. An owl began hooting somewhere in the night, and others joined in. They seemed annoyed with one another, and their hooting grew in volume until their voices disintegrated in shrill screams of anger. The life of some small creature ended with a whimper and a splash not too far away. I had heard the sound before; the last rabbit I ever shot, back in Iowa, made the same cry when I picked it up. There's terror all around us in the darkness, I thought as I drifted off again.

In the morning we could see our breath. There was a patch of ice where I had splashed water on the pier while doing the supper dishes. Catbirds hopped and mewed in the bushes around us, and we could see, for the first time, our site: We were on the edge of Maul Hammock Lake, a pond really. The morning swamp seemed calm, the terror of the night before dispersed by the golden light.

After coffee and oatmeal we set out again, and soon entered dense forest. Now the trail was like a tunnel, with shafts of sunlight piercing the gloom. Often it was so narrow the canoes could barely make the turns. We would back up to maneuver past cypress knees and downed logs, prodding and pushing our way through.

"This is less like paddling than poling," said Sam.

"Is this where push comes to shove?" Toni asked.

That afternoon we came through what may be the prettiest part of the swamp, a narrow lake called Big Water. Canoeing, you enter it quietly. Cypress trees with exposed roots the size of fire hoses rise upward from the inky water, said to be the most reflective in the world. Though the tannin-darkened water is pure enough to drink, the black peat bottom acts as a perfect mirror backing. Spanish moss hangs in clusters from the branches and also—in the water and in full color—from upside-down trees. Clouds, impossibly distant but right at your fingertips, slide beneath the canoe. In one of the trees four or five white egrets sit in upper branches. One of them sees you, hops into space, spreads its wings at the last moment. The others depart as if at a signal, the *whish whish* of their wings the only sound. The sky above and the water below are filled with grace and beauty.

The water also oozes menace. From the muddy shores, from clumps of matted sedge and grasses and roots, from all around you, alligators nearly as black as the water watch you pass with their cool, unblinking eyes. Sinister creatures, they range in size from a couple of feet to monsters. Disconcertingly, they often slither quietly from the shores into the dark water, leaving just their nostrils and knobby eyebrows showing. After a pause, without so much as a ripple, they sink into the reflected clouds. It's as though both water and clouds had suddenly risen over them. I always wondered where the creatures went then, and why, and were they at that moment moving beneath my canoe.

"It's not a good idea to get between gators and their dens," said Toni, "but gators aren't dangerous unless you harass them."

"How do you know where their dens are?" I asked eagerly.

"You don't," she said.

After three days out we canoed into Stephen C. Foster State Park on the western edge of the swamp, our 31-mile trip over. We would take several more, following the winding canoe trails where they led us. Traveling in winter, we missed the spring's profusion of flowers but enjoyed longer vistas through the leafless trees.

The birds made the biggest hit with me. Nowhere in the swamp, it seemed, was there a bird that simply went chirp; they grunted and gurgled, croaked and groaned; they rattled and made barnyard noises—oinks and moos. They managed to sound like rusty hinges and creaky screen doors. Sometimes the white heads of egrets would appear like periscopes above the tall prairie sedge.

The Green canoe trail involves a short portage across Floyds Island, and the campsite there—on dry land—was a respite from the hard wooden platforms. Though I always slept well on them, not everyone does. I awoke one morning to find Sam regarding me coolly. "You look as still and serene as a mummy in your sleeping bag," he said. "I wake up looking like a used Handi-Wipe."

Camped among giant pine trees, with spongy earth beneath us, we sat late around our fire. An overweight raccoon, masked like the bandit it turned out to be, visited camp after supper and made off with a pot holder. We found it, rejected, a few yards away in the morning. Deer peered shyly at us from the woods.

A wooden cabin nearby reminded us that the swamp has been inhabited at various times. "The president of a logging company built it as a hunting lodge back in 1925," said Toni. "The lumbering industry in the Okefenokee started in 1908. There was a railroad that eventually reached 35 miles into the swamp, and millions of board feet of cypress were hauled out. On Billys Island, deep in the swamp, there was a town that held about 600 people." Almost nothing remains of it today. It took just 18 years to clear the swamp of marketable cypress, and the operation halted in 1926.

Leaving Floyds Island we paddled across a prairie, the dry and dusty sedge right at our elbows alongside the narrow trail. Toni was in the bow, Sam somewhere out of sight behind us. Toni and I were both half asleep, drifting along like dust motes in a shaft of sunlight. Suddenly, with an unexpectedness that knocked us both breathless, there beside us was the biggest alligator in the world. A bare paddle-length away and two-thirds the length of the canoe—easily 12 feet long—he was resting in the sun on the grassy bank, immobile as a statue. His eyes were fixed on us, his jaws wide in a toothy grin. Toni and I froze, our paddles in midair, as momentum carried us past. It was awhile before either of us spoke.

"He's dead, right?" said Toni.

"Dead, nothing," I said.

We backed up slowly until we were once again beside him. His corrugated sides moved as he breathed: a stately in-and-out, like a bellows. When he ponderously lifted a hind foot, we moved on.

"Did you know," said Toni as we paddled on, "that young alligators moo like cows?" I didn't know that. "Gators have a muscle in each nostril so they can keep water from getting in their noses." I hadn't known that either. "In addition to fish, alligators eat a lot of waterfowl. They often submerge and wait for a bird to swim by. They grab it by the legs and pull it under and drown it." I wasn't sure how much I wanted to know about that at the moment.

Clay Purvis, a young naturalist-guide at the Okefenokee Swamp Park, gave us more gator stories later. It seems that alligators never hurt anyone in the swamp, though they've been known to gobble dogs. Clay knew of the monster we had seen—"Big Al" we called him. "He's probably 50 or 60 years old," Clay told us. "He's usually there at Floyds Island. Gives everybody a start."

Clay told us about another giant, Oscar, who mostly dozes in the sun near the park center. "This one lady thought Oscar was stuffed. She was just setting her little girl astride him—to take her picture—when we stopped her."

I asked Clay why we hadn't heard any alligators roaring, a sound I had looked forward to hearing. It's a chilling sound, I've been told, a prehistoric roar unchanged from the age of dinosaurs.

"It's too cold now," he said. "Occasionally you'll hear one in winter, but they're most vocal during mating season, in May and

June. If you can't be here then, I'm afraid you'll be disappointed."

A greater disappointment was our failure to work out a fishing date with W. E. ("Preacher") Johnson, an elderly, one-legged black man who was reportedly the best fisherman in the swamp area. We found his home on the outskirts of Folkston, a frame house on a swept and sandy lot with chickens scratching halfheartedly in the hot dust and a hound dog baying and straining at his leash out back.

He made us welcome, took up his crutch, and hobbled over to where his boat—flat-bottomed, aluminum—rested on its trailer. He rummaged around in an overflowing tackle box and pulled out a homemade lure, a tangle of wire and feathers. "Here's what you want," he said. "Them bass, they'll climb in your boat to get at this."

Preacher Johnson works much of the year planting seedlings on a pine plantation, but supplements his income driving canoeists' cars around from one side of the swamp to the other, or toting canoes back and forth. He helped us with car transport several times, but we never managed to find a day when we could all get together for some fishing. He never discouraged us, though. "Any day but Sunday," he would say. "On Sunday I fish for men."

Then Toni had to return to Washington, and Sam and I turned our attention away from the swamp and toward the Suwannee.

Thanks to Stephen Foster, "Suwannee River" looks like a misprint. In 1851 he was writing a new song about the South and needed a two-syllable river name to complete the lyric. "Way down upon the Yazoo River...." Not quite right somehow. "Way down upon the Pedee River." Hmmm. He glanced over a map and spotted the Suwannee. That was it. All he had to do was change the spelling slightly to make it Swanee. But to generations of Americans since then, the Suwannee has looked wrong.

The river's precise origin in the swamp is troublesome, too, but by the time it gets to Griffis Camp, a fishing camp north of Fargo, Georgia, the current is definitely a river. Sam and I chose to start there and follow the Suwannee to the Gulf of Mexico, 230 miles away. At first it was much like paddling through the swamp, the tepid brown water running through a cypress forest.

The current gurgled as it plunged through fallen trees and snags. Turtles slipped from logs into the water a split second before we got a good look at them. Then the forest became less swamplike, with fewer alligators, and by the time we got to Fargo the Suwannee had broad, well-defined banks and recognizable islands.

We camped that night in a roadside park in Fargo, our swamp sounds replaced by those of trucks and cars. Across the highway, a chip mill stayed busy late, conveyors and grapples clashing and growling as they dealt with truckloads of trees. We learned next morning that the mill noise meant logs reduced to chips for papermaking: a 15-year-old pine turned to splinters within six seconds.

That afternoon the winding, narrow river carried us into Florida. Cypress trees, some of them 300-year-old behemoths, stood tall and majestic along the banks. *(Continued on page 62)*

As a May thunderstorm recedes, a canoe trail meanders through Sapling Prairie and into cypress forest; golden club, bright and thick, grows along its margins. Although the trails need cutting twice a year to keep them passable, their routes along natural drainages

conceal man's mark on the Okefenokee. Dense marshland, called prairie because it offers the illusion of grassy plains, constitutes about 15 percent of the swamp. Forests encroach on the prairies, only to retreat again after lightning sets off destructive fires in times of drought.

Two-week-old little blue herons huddle in a nest at the Macks Island rookery. By early June they will leave the nest. Wading birds began nesting here after a small dam flooded the immediate area. Refuge manager John Eadie says: "Habitat and proximity to food source determine where birds nest. But it's a mystery why birds abandon what looks like a good rookery." Above, Arden Griffis, 45, poles his canoe near Macks Island. A fisherman who has lived at the swamp's edge most of his life, he reasons: "Some birds seem to prefer nests over water; they're safer from raccoons there."

Ron's canoe stirs gentle ripples on Minnies Lake in the heart of the swamp as a January sun dips past the cypress forest. "Except for an occasional raucous birdcall or a turtle slipping off a log into the water, it was very quiet in there by day," he recalls. Tannic acid, released by the cypress trees and the dark peat floor of the swamp, enhances the reflective quality of the water. "In a glass or cup, it's the color of tea," says Ron, "but it's absolutely black when you look down into it."

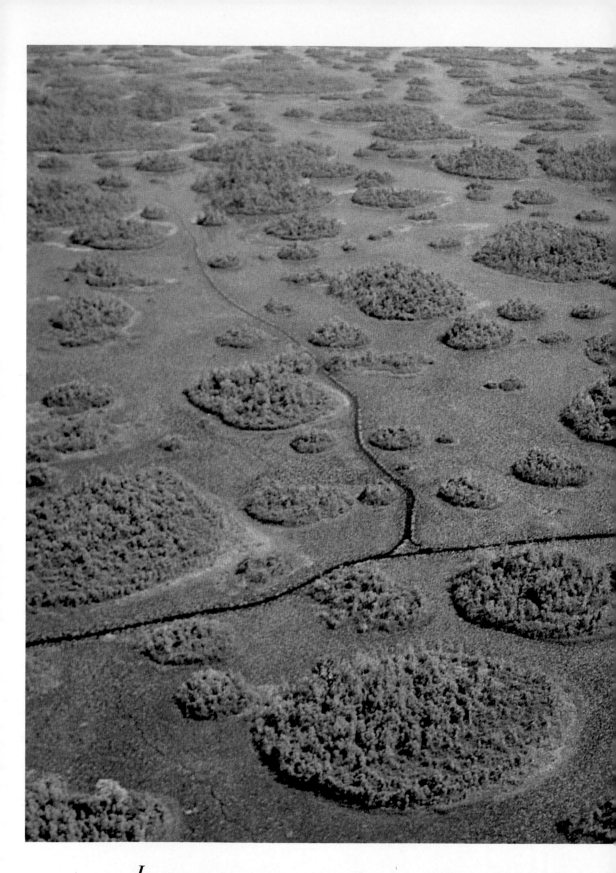

Joined by a canoe trail, the Suwannee River etches a narrow course through Sapling Prairie, about four miles below its source in the northern Okefenokee. The archipelago of "houses" dotting the prairie tells of an ever-changing swamp. Houses, which provide cover

U. S. FISH AND WILDLIFE SERVICE

for wildlife, develop from "batteries," sections of the swamp's peat bottom raised by marsh gas. If a battery endures, grasses, shrubs, and small trees take root, transforming it into a house. Eventually, houses grow and merge to form "bays" — large tracts of cypress.

57

"*The Okefenokee was the most life-filled place we saw on all our travels,*" *says Sam. Of the Cecropia moth at left, he recalls: "I must have watched it on that blade of grass for half an hour. Each time the wind rose I thought it would fly away. But it just opened its wings slowly to stabilize itself." Above, a damselfly rests on a water lily, and an alligator lunges suddenly across sunny shallows. "Entering the swamp was like going far back in geologic time — to a prehistoric world that I had only imagined through books before."*

*L*uminous in the dusk, canoes and a flat-bottomed johnboat used for fishing await another day's riders at Stephen C. Foster State Park. The park, established by the State of Georgia in 1954 and named in honor of the songwriter who immortalized the Suwannee River,

lies at the western entrance to the swamp. There, boats rent for daily travel through the Okefenokee, but camping overnight requires a permit. Five miles downriver, the Suwannee emerges languidly from the swamp and winds 235 miles to the Gulf of Mexico.

"It's nice to see that the loggers missed a few," commented Sam.

There was a good current, a cool breeze, a warm sun. King-fishers swooped down and plucked bugs and minnows from the water. In midafternoon a big fish jumped just under the bow where I was sitting. Its tail thumped the canoe a mighty whack and jangled my thoughts with memories of Oscar and Big Al.

We camped that night on a sandy bank a few feet above the river. Sam built one of his beautiful fires — wood placed just so to burn evenly and well — and after supper we sat with steaming cups of hot chocolate and watched bats dart silently back and forth, snatching mosquitoes out of the air. When Sam went to bed I sat on alone for a while by the waning fire. The idea of a giant alligator crawling up out of the darkness occurred to me, and I frightened myself into moving my sleeping bag farther from the bank.

From the air, the upper Suwannee looks like string spilled on the floor. Its turns and meanders often reversed our direction completely. Once we passed the sound of trucks and bulldozers on our left; a few minutes later they were on the right. About noon of the third day, we glided beneath the highway 6 bridge and nodded "howdies" to some fishermen. Such exchanges never varied much.

"Any luck?"

"Not much. Where'd you put in?"

"Griffis Camp. How far to so and so?"

Fishermen, in boats and on the banks, turned out to be wildly inaccurate on mileages. Ask three fishermen how far it is by river to the nearest town or bridge, and you'll get three different answers — ranging from "just around the next bend" to "oh, 'bout 12 miles." One man said, "about two miles, at the rate you're going." We puzzled over that the rest of the day.

The only bad rapids on the Suwannee are a few miles above White Springs. A sign on shore gives you ample warning. We obeyed a cardinal rule of canoeists — never run a rapid you haven't seen — and stopped for a portage. The river tumbled over a couple of ledges, we saw, dropping about eight feet.

That afternoon the land rolled along beside us, cows mooing in the distance, little sandy roads running down to the river once in a while, chocolate-colored streams joining in at intervals. Now and then we would pick up our paddles, lean back, and just float, feeling very much a part of the river. A blacksnake rustled in the leaves on a steep bank, and had quite a scramble to get up it. A hawk crying overhead — a piteous, lost sound — stopped when it saw us, circled, and disappeared.

We noticed more litter than on previous trips: white Styrofoam ice chests floating along, empty cans, a gas range tumbled down the bank, and the inevitable tire stuck in the mud.

Approaching White Springs, we could hear the soft strains of "Jeanie With the Light Brown Hair" on the bells of a carillon: a memorial to Stephen Foster. Manicured grounds, especially striking after the chaotic tangles of swamp and riverbank, surround the carillon and a museum of Foster memorabilia. Inside, mechanical dioramas illustrate his songs: A steamboat slowly plies the Suwannee; horses thunder down the stretch in the "Camptown Races."

Long ago, Indians—including the famous Seminole chief Osceola—came here for the waters of the spring. Later, visitors from all over the country followed; hotels and boardinghouses sprang up—the Hamilton boasted open fires, electric bells, 4,000 feet of verandas. Sam and I sought out the remains of a four-story wooden structure that had surrounded the spring, its balconies overlooking the water. Sam had seen it as a child, traveling with his parents; "I remember it as being much bigger," he said, bemused.

As we left, another carillon concert was in progress. Its first notes: "Way Down Upon the Swanee River." "Nobody's gonna believe this," I warned Sam. We drifted with the current for as long as the clear birdlike tones reached us through the forest.

Springs give the Suwannee much of its character. Soft limestone, honeycombed with channels, underlies much of this area; spring waters rise from it to join the river, at first running clear, cool, and separate, then slowly blending in. Sulphur—smelly, but once considered healthful—tinges the air near Suwannee Springs; we camped there near abandoned cottages, their windows gone, their porches sagging, relics of a time when wealthy citizens came to bathe in the therapeutic waters.

A couple of days later we canoed into the Suwannee River State Park near Ellaville. Sam went back to finish some photography in the swamp while I went on with another partner. At

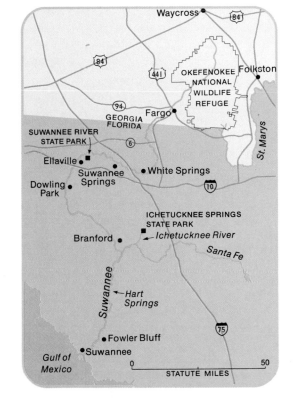

Draining from the swamp, fed by rain and springs, the Suwannee River traces a lazy path southwest through Florida. Proposed in 1974 for preservation under the Wild and Scenic Rivers Act, the Suwannee remained unprotected in 1977.

Folkston I had met Johnny Lloyd, who worked at a truck-stop gas-station restaurant across the highway from my motel. A soft-spoken, muscular young good ol' boy from nearby Homeland, Johnny agreed to accompany me. He promised fresh-caught fish on the way; luckily we had other food along. Shy of manner, at least with new acquaintances, Johnny wouldn't say much except to point out things of interest along the way—which made him a congenial partner for a canoe trip. Soon after we set out he called my attention to a pileated woodpecker—a "wood cock," Johnny said—working in a dead tree about thirty feet up. A big black-and-white bird with a flaming red crest, it would hammer for a bit, reach in and munch something, give a kind of chortling cry, hammer some more.

We had left with a discouraging forecast. Rain was promised — and indeed it had been raining. The river was higher, the water black and roiling, eddies licking the shores. But higher water on the Suwannee means a faster current: good news to a canoeist.

Potential campsites were few and far between now, so we were glad to reach a hamlet called Dowling Park, where a pleasant clearing overlooked the river. After supper a man in a new pickup stopped to chat. He envied our trip.

"My wife won't go camping with me," he told us, "and I don't like to go by myself. Just after we were married we bought a lot of camping equipment and we went once, but while we were sitting by the fire I made the mistake of telling her a story of my grandmother's. It was about a ghost — Scatterbones, a skeleton who rode a skeleton horse — and it scared her (and me, a little) and she made me pack up and take her home. I haven't been camping since then."

Next day Johnny and I heard something scarier: a tornado watch in effect. We kept an eye on the horizon as well as on the river. Below Dowling Park the Suwannee widens, and slows. More vacation homes appear on the banks, more "No Trespassing" signs. A couple of carpenters, building a new house, watched us pass with melancholy smiles. "What a life," one of them called.

I thought of him when the wind and the rain came. We could see the squalls coming toward us. When they hit, I've found, there's nothing to do but lower your head, grit your teeth, and squint your eyes. I would rather spend rainy days paddling — however wet I get — than cooped up in a tent or hunkered down in the mud around a smoldering fire. So we kept going, our jeans soaked, the tarp across the cargo flapping in the wind. It rained all afternoon, and sometimes it was a deluge. I thought of the old spiritual — "Didn't it rain, now children, didn't it rain." Rainwater sloshed over our feet, and we sweated uncomfortably inside our ponchos. What a life. Mercifully, we escaped a tornado; the wind, though strong, was at our backs. After paddling 37 miles we reached Branford about 7 p.m. — a record for mileage I've never beaten since.

The next day we stopped at Hart Springs, one of the larger ones along the river. On the average, fifty million gallons of water a day flow from it into the Suwannee — at a constant 72° F. temperature. We paddled across a little sand reef and up the stream. Its water, a pale green, was amazingly clear; we could see largemouth bass swimming about listlessly. I remembered Preacher Johnson's lure, and decided that even he couldn't have caught them.

For the end of our trip the winter weather turned beautiful: hot days, warm nights, cloudless skies. The river widened more. The landscape, flat and marshy, was brilliant with water birds: herons and egrets, ibises and cranes. Piers reached out toward us from most of the cottages; we saw more and more fishermen's boats, powerboats, bigger and faster ones.

Our last night out we camped at Fowler Bluff — a little town with a low shoreline—amidst a storm of sand gnats. Below this point the river became a lazy lake, its shores half a mile away.

"We're within the reach of the tide now," Johnny said. "Somebody who boats down here a lot could probably notice it, but I can't." Neither could I.

Near the mouth of the river we were like minnows in a school of sharks as big oceangoing cabin cruisers seemed to do their best to swamp us. The swash of their wakes would send us heeling over wildly. I decided that I had wasted a lot of worry on alligators; these boats were the worst hazard yet. More than once I thought I might hear some Southern cussin'; but Johnny, who coached basketball teams for his church, remained calm and self-possessed. All he ever said was, "The sons-o'-guns apparently don't realize they're supposed to slow down when they pass a canoe." We hadn't seen any other canoes on the river, which supported his theory.

On the coast, we found the town of Suwannee devoted to boating: power boating. There were more marinas than gas stations. Here Sam met us, to take us north by car.

Much later I learned that plenty of people along the Suwannee associate canoes with outsiders—the sort of outsiders who talk a lot about ecology and want the federal government to regulate the river. In 1974 the Department of the Interior proposed to make it a Wild and Scenic River under the law, limiting development and home building and such. This would not have met all the problems of pollution from strip mining for phosphate in the limestone country upriver, but it would have controlled lesser projects along the banks. Property owners, with their vacation cottages in mind, resented the idea of any interference. Some folks even thought that Interior's proposal meant changing "Suwannee" to "Wild"—"how'd you like to have Washington rename *your* river?" Those sons-o'-guns in powerboats had kept up speed on purpose.

I guess the Southerners we met just hadn't heard about all that.

Wooden shelter juts from a peaceful cove along the swamp's 96-mile canoe-trail system. Four such structures, built since 1970, now allow canoeists to camp overnight within the bounds of the refuge.

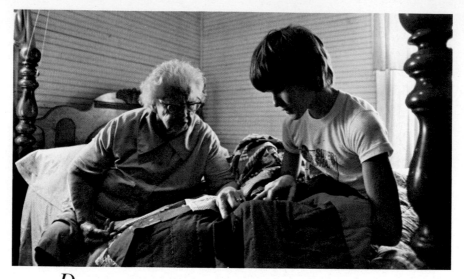

*D*awn breaks on a quiet bend in the Suwannee River near White Springs. "I've been here for 46 years; it's good here," says Sarah Touchton, 83, of her home on the river near Fargo, Georgia. "Granny Sarah"—as her neighbors know her—tells her grandson Clay Mitchell, 12, about a quilt she has made him. Below, Jake Colson, 45, of Suwannee, Florida, sets out to lay turtle traps near the river's mouth. A sturgeon fisherman and a crabber as well, he says: "My life comes from the water."

Carefree on a summer afternoon, children float down the clear and cold Ichetucknee River near Branford, Florida. Rising through limestone in Ichetucknee Springs State Park, the river flows 4¹/₂ miles before entering the Santa Fe, which then feeds the Suwannee. One

day in July 1976, almost 4,700 people made this journey in rafts and inner tubes. "There's just too much congestion," says state naturalist Jim Stevenson; "it's hurting plant and animal life along the river." The state now intends to limit daily use of the Ichetucknee.

3

On Heartland Waters: Three Varied Streams

TRANSPARENT GREEN WATER SWEPT BENEATH THE BRIDGE, a simple concrete slab above the Buffalo River in Arkansas. The current carried with it fragments of dark leaves and twigs, tumbling and turning them in the rushing stream. Its depth would decide the timing for the first of our three trips in the nation's heartland, on tributaries of the Mississippi system.

"If the water were just a couple inches lower we wouldn't go," said John McRaven. This young canoeist was to be my sternman during our overnight, 24-mile trip from the Ponca bridge down to Pruitt. "Up here near the headwaters the water level varies widely during the year," he added, kicking a pebble into the stream. "We use the Ponca bridge as a gauge. If there's more than 19 inches of air between the bridge and the water, the river's too low for good canoeing. You'll spend a lot of time wading and dragging your canoe through riffles and across gravel bars. If the water's a foot or so over the bridge, it's too high for safe canoeing—or driving either." We had a slight margin: about 16 inches of air.

The Buffalo begins its 148-mile length in the Boston Mountains within the Ozark National Forest. It runs east to its junction with the White River, which in turn empties into the Mississippi. The upper six miles, between Boxley and Ponca, are generally too shallow and rough for canoeing.

In 1963 a National Park study declared the Buffalo to be "nationally significant," and—after a dam scare that came to a head in 1964—it became the first National River by Act of Congress in 1972. As such it enjoys even greater protection than units in the National Wild and Scenic Rivers System. It should run undammed

Plucked from the clear waters of the Buffalo, a baby turtle paddles the air. Botany student Doug Gosling, who joined Ron and Sam in the Ozarks, returned the turtle to the river.

OZARK

MISSOURI
ARKANSAS

ARKANSAS
OKLAHOMA

PLATEAU

65

62

Bull Shoals
Lake

Dam

Yellville

Hemmed-in
Hollow

Big Bluff

Fayetteville

Lost Valley

Ponca

Boxley

Camp
Orr

Pruitt

Buffalo
Point

Buffalo

BUFFALO
NATIONAL
RIVER

White

62

16

71

7

14

65

Boston Mountains

0   50
STATUTE MILES

America's first National River, so designated in 1972, the Buffalo flows undisturbed by man —one of a dwindling number of undammed streams in the 48 states. It runs 148 miles in a near-wilderness of hills and hollows, forests and meadows, before it joins the White in Arkansas.

indefinitely. More than ten million people live within 250 miles of the Buffalo, but the river itself moves through solitude, the domain of birds and beavers, wild flowers and forested gorges.

There were six of us in three canoes—friends and relatives of John's—setting out that morning from the Ponca bridge. A lead-mining center in World War I, Ponca is nearly deserted now. Often its 40-some residents are outnumbered by canoe parties. We had camped a little way downstream the night before—with lightning flickering in the south and beavers slapping the water—and we awoke to bird songs in the sweet gums and willows along the banks.

The willows are one of the hazards of the upper Buffalo. They lean out over the water like whisk brooms and can easily sweep a paddler out of his craft and into the water. The rapids are numerous and fast, but small and generally easy to negotiate.

Canoeists often refer to an international scale of difficulty for rapids. It begins with Class (or Grade) I: "Moving water with a few riffles and small waves. Few or no obstructions." Class III is not for beginners: "Rapids with high, irregular waves often capable of swamping an open canoe. Narrow passages that often require complex maneuvering. May require scouting from shore." Class V involves "significant hazard to life in event of a mishap." Class VI is the end: "Difficulties of Class V carried to the extreme of navigability. Nearly impossible and very dangerous. For team of experts only after close study and with all precautions taken." We would encounter nothing more serious than Class II ("easy rapids") on the Buffalo, though some of the rapids at bends approached Class III.

My river-running education began almost as soon as we set off. I learned that piloting a canoe on a fast river isn't at all like driving a car on a freeway, though the comparison seems logical at first. Just because the bow of a canoe is partly to the left you aren't necessarily achieving a course to the left—it can mean that the current is swinging you broadside and making you a bigger target for boulders downstream. To round a bend, simply keeping the canoe aligned with the current won't do it. A captive of the current, you'll simply bump along against the outside bank of the stream.

A number of strokes — backs and draws and prys and braces — are especially important for a canoeist negotiating fast water. Many are designed to move a canoe to left or right across the current so it can take the safest route while avoiding broadside hazards.

The back stroke is just that: used when you want to back up or stop headway. And there were plenty of times when I wanted to! A draw stroke pushes water beneath the canoe, thereby "drawing" the canoe toward the paddle. It's often a last-minute maneuver for avoiding an obstacle. In contrast, a pry stroke moves or pries the canoe away from the paddle. A brace is used to steady the canoe or to prevent capsizing. John worked on all the strokes with me as we progressed down the Buffalo.

"Draw!" he would call as we careened around a bend, sliding ominously toward a limb hung with dangling willow branches.

"Pry!" he would shout as a boulder loomed before us.

Our destination for the night was Camp Orr, a Boy Scout camp 12 miles downstream. "The river drops 145 feet in those 12 miles," John told me, "enough to make for an exciting ride." Often we could see only the heads and shoulders of the canoeists in front of us as they slid out of sight down perceptible slopes.

We passed Big Bluff that morning — a sheer limestone cliff more than 500 feet high, on our left. We stopped and hiked in to a well-known beauty spot for lunch. This is Hemmed-in Hollow, a three-sided bowl of rock with a 200-foot waterfall that tumbles over one edge and disintegrates as it falls, reaching the base as spray or mist. "It's the highest waterfall in the Ozarks," John remarked, pointing out ferns clinging to the walls.

"People have lived along the Buffalo for 9,000 years," he told me. "The first inhabitants were hunters and gatherers, but as agriculture developed they built villages in the bottoms. They also used caves under the bluffs. Archeologists have catalogued more than 250 sites along the river."

We camped that night on a gravel bar just below the Boy Scout base — steaks for supper, fresh meat and vegetables being one of the bonuses of short trips — and continued the next day to our take-out point at Pruitt. The river during this stretch drops just 8½ feet per mile, so the current was considerably slower, and the shoals and rapids were farther apart.

Several times we passed through clouds of fragrance and looked up to find a clump of pink wild azaleas clinging to a bluff. In the clear water the moss-covered rocks on the bottom slid beneath us like wraiths, and water snakes wriggled across the chilly river before us. It made me wonder if one side of the river really offers them more than the other. As we passed they would hoist their heads another inch out of the water, the better to see us.

Beaver sign was thick along the banks — willows chopped off a few inches above the ground, sticks cleaned of their bark. Tooth marks looked like embossed patterns on the white branches. One beaver swimming upstream through a fast riffle made it look easy.

I heard some details of local history from John's brother Charles, the "Mac" of the family, and Mac's wife, Linda. Mac, a writer and formerly a teacher, had gone to Ponca about ten years ago "to write and get away from it all" and eventually decided that he had gotten *too* far away. "It must have been fairly lively when the mines were open," he explained, "and people could make some money taking in miners as roomers, but now it doesn't even have a store. People at Ponca have their own gardens, cattle, and hogs.

"The only business at Ponca is Lost Valley Lodge, which used to be the truck-garage facility for the mines; I converted the last garage into an apartment, by the way, back in '68, and now it's called the Ozark Room. The nearest thing to a local industry is driving canoeists' cars from Ponca down to a take-out point, at Camp Orr or Pruitt. One of the local fellows drives his own car so he can run the others back to Ponca."

Pruitt today consists of a ranger station. Its location, where state highway 7 crosses the river, made it more of a center 25 years ago. Then it had a couple of motels and a store that catered to fishing parties, but it was always a very small town.

"You find these little 'place-name places' where villages were, about every five miles," said Mac. "That was a good day's journey, up and down these hills."

Settlement came late to the immediate vicinity of the Buffalo. Generally speaking, the soils were rocky, the valleys narrow.

"People went into the hills during the Depression," said Linda, "to put up a cabin and try to raise some vegetables and keep chickens or hogs. But they would leave again as soon as they thought they could make a living outside. You can go hiking near the river with the feeling that you're in untouched wilderness, and then you come to a place with five or six foundations where the houses have fallen down or burned. People must have really scratched to survive." It's pretty country by her account — but pretty desolate.

Boxley is an exception, not only beautiful but also fertile and spacious. As Linda put it, Boxley isn't exactly a town; it's a valley with houses, a wide valley by local standards. As much as a quarter mile across, it offers enough sunny ground for gardens to do well, and more than 60 people live there, with two stores to shop at. A major landowner and recognized matriarch is Mrs. Orphea Duty.

She has lived in the same house at Boxley for 67 of her 78 years, tending beds of irises in the summer, quilting in the winter, and feeding banana-nut bread to the birds. "They like raisin pie pretty well, too," she says. A Tupperware dealer for 14 years, she still covers five counties in northern Arkansas. In 1962 she traveled to Washington, D. C., to testify before a Senate committee against the proposed Buffalo dam. Its lake would not have reached her land, but she preferred the river as it was.

To see the Buffalo down to its junction with the White, Sam and I put together another group. It included Doug Gosling, who had studied English with Sam when he taught high-school classes

Sweet-gum leaf, sharp green in spring or gold to reddish-purple in autumn, impressed Ron and Sam in the Ozarks. At waterside the tree may reach a height of more than 100 feet.

in Ohio and had traveled with Sam on the Pacific Crest Trail. After our trip, our guide had serious trouble involving a state alcohol agent; I'll call him Tex, because he wore a Western-style hat and cowboy boots. In these he was an incongruous canoeist; he had spent most of his time on the river in the square-nosed motorboats favored by fishing parties, whom he had been guiding for years. He certainly knew the Buffalo, and he promised me I would catch some fish on this trip, a by-now-familiar refrain.

As we glided along, he scanned the bottom constantly. He would point with his paddle: "There'll be a brownie under that rock." A couple of casts later he would have a brown bass alongside the canoe. Once he spotted a two-pound bass in the water: "It'll only take a second to catch him." He used four minnows and got a couple of strikes—once working the fish to within a few inches of the canoe before it broke free. "That's the last time he'll bite," he said. "He won't chase another minnow till he gets mighty hungry."

"The Buffalo's like an Interstate Highway," Tex told us. "There's a lot of money spent along it—outfitters, guides, fishing trips, organizers all depend on the river for their incomes."

Nevertheless, like many of his neighbors, he felt some resentment toward the bureaucrats who manage the river and the flocks of out-of-state fishermen who deplete its waters. "There's so many fishermen now the fish don't have time to grow. Used to be you could get twenty or thirty catfish out of the Buffalo in one day. No more." His little six-year-old daughter had just been presented with her first rod and reel, and Tex was looking forward to taking her fishing the following weekend—even a small fish would give her something grand to remember.

As we made our way slowly down the Buffalo—winding among verdant hills and bluffs, the Arkansas sun warm and gentle, the birds "hollerin'" as Tex put it—canoeing lived up to its reputation as an ideal way of enjoying an area. There was seldom a time when we couldn't hear at least two different kinds of birds singing, see a dozen tints of green in the forested hills, smell wild flowers in bloom, watch the water dance across a riffle. Occasionally a minnow would go skimming across the surface like a skipped rock, a big black shadow right behind it. We camped on gravel bars, dined on catfish, zipped ourselves snugly into the tents during nighttime showers when lightning exploded outside like flashbulbs, and awoke early to see puffs of mist moving downstream with the current.

We saw a few other canoe parties. One couple had a puppy that scampered back and forth across their cargo. Another canoe carried two teenage boys, the sternman distressingly fat; the bow of that canoe was two inches out of the water.

We saw a lot of fishermen, mostly in outfitted, guided parties. Once a commissary boat, coming along fast, rounded a bend just upstream of our campsite, and an overhanging branch plucked the driver right out of the boat and knocked him straight over backward into the river. The boat roared on empty. *(Continued on page 82)*

At one of the Buffalo's well-known gravel-bar campsites, river mist mingles with valley fog in early morning; it veils the greens of sycamore and ash, gum, witch hazel, and willow on the hillsides. Near the tent Doug Gosling folds his poncho. The party's guide takes

a last cup of coffee from Ron. "We lingered around the campfire hating to see breakfast end," says Ron. "We knew it would take more than an hour of hard work and hassle to get all the provisions and gear jammed into packs and loaded securely in the canoes."

*P*ointing out a favorite iris, Orphea Duty gardens near the home she has lived in for 67 years at Boxley. Downriver at the Buffalo Point recreation area, a skilled canoeist gives paddling tips to an out-of-state novice. Such visitors often come to the river by way of Yellville, where neighbors catch up on local news outside the Marion County Courthouse.

WALTER MEAYERS EDWARDS

*On the face of Big Bluff, highest cliff in the Ozarks, a hiker stops
to rest along Goat Trail, named for the feral stock that runs free in
the area. More than 300 feet below, Ron and his party floated down the
Buffalo's meanders through pastureland. "We decided to stop for lunch about
three miles downstream from here," says Ron, "and after banking the canoes
we hiked north to Hemmed-in Hollow to see the waterfall." Highest free-
leaping waterfall between the southern Appalachians and the Rockies, it
plunges down 200 feet past crumbling ledges of limestone and breaks into
spray before hitting the valley floor. "The water weaves and curls as the
wind blows," says Ron; "it's beautiful. And after walking half a mile we
were tempted to try a midday shower, clothes and all."*

The driver struggled to run it down, splashing through knee-deep water and hollerin' mightily. It was just as well, I thought, that this wasn't a day for a riverside baptizing. Finally the boat ran itself onto a bank, its motor still whining and churning, and the driver reached it, still hollerin'.

As for the fishing, I did my best. I thought I was going to catch one little bass. Tex pointed her out to me. She was just visible in the shadow of a large flat rock. I cast a few times, trying to tempt her with a minnow. Finally, I succeeded in placing the by-now-dead minnow just a few inches from her nose. The bass regarded it with interest. She ventured out, fastidiously picked it up by the tail, moved it a couple of feet downstream, let go of it, and returned to her nest. I was bowled over by this, and played the game with her for half an hour. Sometimes she moved the carcass downstream, sometimes up, but always with a gentle resolve to keep the litter away from her door.

Snakes and turtles were sunning themselves along the banks. "A turtle is like a compost heap," Doug told me. "The sun on their shells helps them digest their food." We came across one the size of a pie pan, balanced on its stomach on the stump of a branch, all four feet in the air. As we approached, it made frantic swimming motions, and finally it toppled inelegantly onto its back in the river.

Bright red cardinals flitted in the forest, and bobwhites called their names across the ridges. A bluff we passed housed a flock of cooing pigeons. A group of turkey vultures—looking like monks in black habits—scavenged a deserted campsite as we passed; the fire was still smoking. Whippoorwills often sang in the night. One evening we heard a hound dog howling far away; it wasn't coon-hunting season, but he might have been after a fox.

At one camp Sam found a beetle and a baby turtle locked in combat. His sympathies were with the turtle. The beetle had it by a hind leg, had dragged it far from water, had injured its left eye. Sam rescued the turtle and set it gently in a shallow eddy. It stayed there, rubbing its eye with a tiny webbed foot.

Our last day out, we hurried to beat a rainstorm. Thunder and lightning were right behind us as we entered the White River. We paddled hard—very hard—against the surging river to a boat ramp on the north bank half a mile upstream. As we loaded the canoes onto our car, the rain began. We were doubly glad to be off the White. At any time the power station upstream at Bull Shoals Dam might release water enough to raise the level of the river eight feet or more—enough to sweep a canoe away like one of the Buffalo's tumbling leaves.

A proposed dam on a little creek in Indiana would sweep away a good deal more. We loaded our gear and drove to Indiana to investigate, and nearly succeeded in drowning the dam's chief opponent in the very creek she was trying to save.

Wildcat Creek flows westward across central Indiana; its three branches unite and join the Wabash just above Lafayette, home of

Purdue University. The 1965 Federal Flood Control Act authorized a dam on the Wildcat 7.2 miles upstream from its mouth. The resulting reservoir, largest in the valley, was to serve flood control, water quality, fish and wildlife conservation, and recreation; its area would vary between 3,220 acres and 9,580 acres at "full pool." The dam—one of 29 that the U. S. Army Corps of Engineers has built or recommended for the Wabash basin—would be 3,540 feet long, 149 feet high, and cost $110,000,000.

One of its most influential supporters has been David C. Pfendler, an administrator in Purdue's School of Agriculture from 1939 to 1974. A friend compares his features to the late Sir Winston Churchill's and his tenacity to a bulldog's. Dean Pfendler took an active role in stressing conservation long before ecology became a campaign issue, and he stresses the harm man has done to the Wabash basin. Settlers cut the virgin forests and plowed up the prairie grasses until the rivers turned muddy and subject to flooding; human and industrial wastes added pollution. "The Indian word *Wahb* meant something like 'white' or 'crystal,'" he says. "It has been a long time since the Wabash deserved a name like that."

Clean-up efforts began about a decade ago. Dean Pfendler comments: "Any fool can stand at a sewer mouth and yell 'foul.' Only teams of trained scientists and trained engineers can be effective in improving this situation. The massive degradation of the Wabash Valley was reversed by large engineering projects, and it will be carried forward only by massive projects that are a carefully chosen part of an integrated whole."

As such, the Wildcat dam appealed to many for a time. Among them were members of Purdue's famous engineering schools; a water-quality specialist for a pharmaceutical firm; executives of a corn-processing plant downriver; the Republican mayor of West Lafayette and the Democratic mayor of Lafayette.

A few years ago Mrs. Joseph Wick—Connie—considered the reservoir scheme and found it bad. The wife of a Christian Church (Disciples of Christ) minister, and mother of three, she has devoted six years and every penny she could lay her hands on to fighting the Lafayette dam. She put together a party of canoeists and kayakers to show us a stretch of the threatened Wildcat. As we coasted along —with Connie a "duffer," or passenger, between Sam and me—she

Wildcat Creek goes rushing westward through farmland and forest in central Indiana. Its three branches unite and join the Wabash above Lafayette. Strong opposition by area residents has halted—at least temporarily—the construction of a dam that would create a lake indicated as a yellow area.

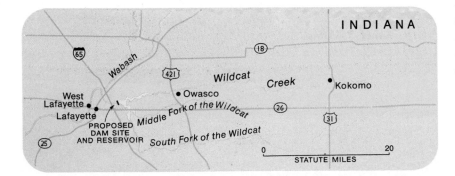

Canoeists glide under a wooden bridge a century old, near Owasco on the Wildcat. Connie Wick, who organized this outing, has also organized citizen opposition to the idea of a reservoir that when full would cover more than 9,000 acres and dramatically alter the character of the stream. Her fight for the Wildcat has won her the nickname "the Colonel." Below, she paints her federation's slogan on the window of her car. Above, an animal track records an early-morning visit to the bank.

talked of the dam and the people involved in the controversy. The stream, though narrow, was deep and fast, and we made good time, rushing along under a canopy of oaks and sycamores.

"The Corps has been talking about a dam in this area since the thirties, but no one took them seriously until 1963. Then a meeting was held here in Lafayette where the Corps presented an interim report in three volumes. *Three volumes!* The city fathers were for it —the bankers, realtors, businessmen.

"In 1975 I helped organize the Wildcat Creek Federation, and we started holding meetings and doing research and putting together people who were willing to work with us. I learned a great deal about the political process. You just find the pressure points and begin pressing them. We've concentrated on the politicians. We persuaded our Congressman, Floyd Fithian, to come around to our point of view, and he's introduced a bill to de-authorize the dam. Unless Congress does that the battle isn't really won.

"Naturally we opposed the dam on environmental grounds— the damage to the area, the loss of wildlife, the number of homes that would be destroyed, all those acres of mudflats between low water and 'full pool.' But it all comes down to economics. About three years ago a friend sat in my living room and said, 'Connie, you've got to get yourself an economist and get the figures. Those people in Washington aren't going to pay any attention to birds and rabbits.' So we did. We figure that as of 1976 there would be a return worth 53 cents for every dollar of public money spent."

As Connie talked, her eyes would flash with anger or grow somber when she spoke of fighting bureaucracy. "We're trying to protect ourselves out of our own pockets against our own government. That's what's driven me more than anything."

We stopped for lunch on a broad grassy bank, and Connie unpacked a picnic lunch: salami and cheese, apples and granola. We ate in the shade of giant oaks, and Connie talked of the private costs of the battle. "You know, most of the proponents of these projects can afford it. They don't give up their vacations because they've pledged $400 to the Wildcat effort this year. Not on your life. It's been harder for us. When the Wildcat Creek Federation went to Washington last year to attend the de-authorization hearings, we took a bus. Those people sat up and rode all night, and rode all night coming back, because it only cost them $36 apiece instead of $152 by plane. A friend of mine says, 'This is why Washington's so slow to respond to little people like us. The only people the politicians see are the ones with enough money to make the trip.'"

After our lunch and a rest in the shade, we took to our canoes again, and the quick current swept us along. "We've had some fun, too," said Connie, trailing her fingers in the water. "We always attend the opposition's meetings—wearing our Stop the Dam buttons—to keep abreast of what they're up to. At a meeting they held on the need for industrial water downstream, I sat beside a shy little man. During the question-and-answer period, he kept timidly try-

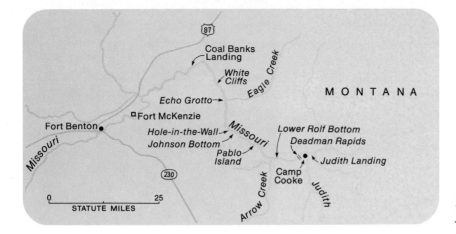

The upper reaches of the Missouri, route to the Northwest, provided passage for trappers and fur traders. Meriwether Lewis and William Clark made their famous journey of discovery here in May and June of 1805.

ing to get the chairman's attention. Finally I said, 'Shoot! Get your hand up there, he'll call on you.' And he said, 'Well, you're not gonna like it. I'm for the reservoir.' And I said, 'That's all right, you've got a right to ask your question. Put your hand up.'

"So finally they called on him, and he stood up and said, 'I'm for this dam, but you better do a better job here than you did down at Raccoon Lake. It's nothing but mud down there.' I couldn't have gotten the point across better if I'd tried. We just howled."

Dean Pfendler served as a leader of "the opposition"—that is, as chairman of a nonprofit organization called "Citizens for Coordinating and Planning Lafayette Lake." Its slogan was straightforward: "Dam Right." Its arguments included this: "I think we ought to control floods, not depend on Washington to bail us out whenever it rains." It stressed the prospect of wages for dam construction, and an expanded tax base in future decades. It also stressed the value of a lake and surrounding greenbelt for local and migratory waterfowl. It emphasized the point that the lake's two-pronged shape would allow separate areas for swimming, fishing, boating and water-skiing—and canoeing.

Debate went on for months, and Dean Pfendler summarizes the local attitudes that affected the outcome: "Farmers saw the business interest of the city dictating to and encroaching upon rural areas, and destroying a way of life. Militant environmentalists could see nothing but short-run environmental disaster. A substantial number of conservatives was against anything that increased the public debt. These groups, along with other support they could generate, were able to defeat the project. Looking back," he concludes, "it seems unbelievable."

As of 1977, it seems certain that the Wildcat will continue to run untamed, through rich farmland and the rolling wooded country that Sam and I saw with Connie and her allies.

As we paddled along, we had been noticing and commenting on the darkening sky, and about midafternoon a storm hit us. The wind began to pick up, sending leaves and twigs whirling through the air, rippling the surface of the creek. When it began to get really bad we pulled over into an eddy by a low bluff, hung on to one another's canoes, and huddled down to sit it out.

That turned out to be the nearest thing to a tornado I've ever been in, and indeed tornadoes were reported in Indiana that afternoon. Winds from a black sky roared across us, bowing the trees and hurling branches down around us. After the winds came the rain, refreshing at first, then cold. We put on ponchos and life jackets for warmth, and when the storm slacked off we started on.

Just a few minutes later, trouble struck. Rounding a bend, we bumped up against a barely submerged tree limb, and our canoe turned sideways in the stream. Instinctively we leaned sideways —leaning upstream, the wrong way—and over we went.

The American Whitewater Affiliation has assembled a list of do's and don'ts for canoeists. Under the heading "If You Spill" the last recommendation is "BE CALM, but don't be complacent." (Calmness I can sometimes achieve, but complacency I've never even approached.) In this case, though the water was deep and fast, we were able to keep a grip on the canoe—which was still stuck on the limb—and work our way along it until we got everyone ashore.

But the canoe stayed where it was, full of water, pressed against the limb by the current. In a 5-mile-per-hour current, an 18-foot canoe full of water will press against whatever it's up against with a force of more than 2,500 pounds. Which is why you never want to get pinned between a swamped canoe and a boulder. It's like the saying, "Whether the rock hits the pitcher, or the pitcher hits the rock, it's going to be bad for the pitcher."

So our canoe stayed firmly lodged—making ominous cracking sounds—despite our best efforts. Finally, with a rope tied to the bow and all of us tugging hard, we managed to haul it ashore.

Tired and wet and cold, we got back to Connie's none the worse for our unexpected swim. Over hot coffee I asked the question I had been wondering about all day: "Why you, Connie? Why are you the one who's fighting this battle?"

Splashing through island shallows, a white-tailed doe flees from the author's presence. She gives the danger signal of the species—holding the tail raised and displaying tufts of white rump hair.

She fixed upon me the gaze that made bureaucrats quake: "There's a line in the Talmud that my husband often quotes. 'Where there is no man, strive thou to be that man.' That's why."

A remarkable woman, I thought, as we left Indiana and the frolicsome Wildcat for another journey on free-running water.

This would take us along one of the last undammed segments of the upper Missouri River. Sam's cousin Craig Lockwood joined us, and with us went another remarkable woman, a young historian for the Bureau of Land Management in Montana. Edrie Vinson has studied the Missouri extensively, seems to know every inch of it, and loves to share it with visitors. We met her in late summer at Fort Benton, Montana, a town that grew up at a trading post in the 1840's, and there we made arrangements for a week-long canoe trip. We would cover one of the river's most historic stretches, from Coal Banks Landing to Judith Landing, 46 miles downstream.

On an overcast day we drove to our put-in point, named for a dark seam of low-quality coal showing on the left bank. "The steamboats tried to use it for fuel when the trees had all been cut down," Edrie said, "but it's too poor to burn." Gray, eroded slopes edged the river, with white sandstone terraces showing here and there; the aroma of fresh sage—a 'kitcheny' smell—rose from miles and miles of stubby sagebrush.

We loaded our canoes, but Craig noticed water seeping into the bottom of one. Rough treatment was catching up with the canvas. "Wood-and-canvas canoes will need repairing," a canoe-loving colleague once remarked, "but when you have calm water and good scenery—like those white cliffs on the Missouri—you don't want aluminum. You don't want to hear the paddle *clunk clunk clunk* on the gunwale. You want to hear the stillness. That's what it's all about." Craig did a patch job with glue and tape, quickly and efficiently, and off we went.

This far up, the Missouri is fast and narrow, not the broad giant it becomes farther down. It runs through country known as the Missouri Breaks, which is broken terrain, sharply eroded,with steep slopes and coulees wearing back from the waterside. Bluffs along the river were caked with the cone-shaped mud nests of cliff swallows; they looked like miniature mud huts. On one of the cutbanks, Edrie pointed out the remains of a prehistoric fire pit and a fire-cracked rock, once the site of an Indian camp or settlement. Whitened bison bones—ribs and legs and toothy jaws—protruded from the muddy bank.

This stretch of the Missouri has witnessed several waves of American life, ranging from the Indians of prehistory to the 20th-century homesteaders. Lewis and Clark made their historic exploration through this country; fur traders followed them; and steamboats and soldiers followed in their turn.

With steamboats came the woodhawks, men who supplied fuel. Cottonwood was the most plentiful, and commonly used even though it didn't really burn very well. Rosin or tar—or even spoiled sowbelly—was thrown into the furnace to help generate steam. When the trees had all been cleared from along the river, the woodhawks took to tearing down abandoned houses or sheds or trading posts; so today little physical evidence of the early settlers and river posts remains.

It sometimes seemed that Edrie had a story for every mile we traveled. We passed a long string of beautiful big cottonwoods on our right. "There were no trees at all left when John Isaacson homesteaded this land in 1901," she said. "He was a Norwegian with a wife and two sons. One of his sons took it upon himself to plant cottonwoods along the bank to make it look as it had before. He carried one bucket of water for every tree for years. You see the result." There must have been a hundred trees standing in a line along the bank, majestic in full leaf.

The big cottonwoods of the bottomland, I learned later, had been ideal for making dugout canoes in the early days. Boats up to 30 feet long were hewed from the immense trunks, their ends built up slightly to create a bow and stern, partitions left in place every four to six feet to provide strength. Such craft served mainly for the comings and goings around the river posts, though messengers also used them for fast trips to St. Louis.

A little later we stopped to examine four old structures of varying age. One had been little more than a woodhawk's den, dug into the earth, its wooden roof collapsed and bleached; another, a frame house built in the 1930's as a lineshack for herders. It faced a glorious view across the river—a skyline of pinnacles and peaks—but had no windows on that side, probably to escape the cross-river winds. Another cabin was reduced to a mere cottonwood foundation. The last building had been more elaborate: a stone-lined cellar; cottonwood logs; sawed boards. Only the buzzing of insects disturbed the silence.

Later, as we rounded a bend, Edrie rested her paddle across her lap. "Here, in Civil War times, a group of renegade whites—dressed up like Indians—attacked a steamboat heading down to St. Louis with gold worth $250,000. They must have had a small cannon. From that bluff up there"—she pointed to the left—"they shot the boat's stacks over, forcing her to beach. They got the gold, but were caught later and hanged by a party out of Fort Benton. When the water's clearer, you can see the outline of the boat from up on the bluff. But people say the gold was never recovered."

Edrie had us beach the canoes later where a low canyon wound inland, its flanks supporting patches of grasses and stunted shrubs. We hiked to a spot where white outcrops of limestone rose around the remains of a cabin. "Jack Munro built it—of fieldstone and cut limestone—about 1890," she said. A recognizable doorway remained, but the white walls were crumbling heaps.

"Those walls were more than a foot thick," Edrie said. "Munro was a stonemason by trade, but he made his living rustling horses. He never corralled them, but let hundreds run loose in the breaks.

Every once in a while he would round up a herd and run them east to Miles City to sell. He supposedly built several stone cabins along the river." No doubt those thick stone walls were useful if a posse showed up.

Munro was no isolated rustler. Stealing horses and cattle was practically an industry in the area for a while. Stockmen in 1883 estimated that they lost three percent of their herds to rustlers. Sam McKenzie, a Scotch half-breed, stole horses in Montana, ran them to Canada where he sold them, stole more horses up there, and brought them back and sold them at Fort Benton.

We camped that night at Eagle Creek, in the very spot where Lewis and Clark had camped on May 31, 1805. We could imagine the presence of long-departed souls, and Edrie could tell stories of many lives long ended: "Indians lived all about here. You can still find drive lines where they hunted bison and antelope, and butchering sites, and places where men worked on spearpoints or arrowheads. And steamboats landed their upstream freight here during low water; wagon trains would carry it on to Fort Benton. Blackfeet and Piegan Indians attacked one train in 1869 and killed one of the crew."

Across the river we had stopped at Echo Grotto—a natural bowl that reminded me of Hemmed-in Hollow without greenery—and seen the word "Mandan" painted in lampblack on one of the walls. "In the 1870's Congress appropriated funds to clear the Missouri channel," Edrie explained. "The U.S.S. *Mandan* went to work on it in the '80's. Her base was right here at Eagle Creek; a crewman painted her name over at the grotto. She swamped here in 1910 when the crew failed to get her ashore before the ice locked her in."

Next day we came upon rough water—as this stretch went—from a school of little fish. A couple of dozen of them made the water dance as they surfaced, flipped a fin, ate something—and vanished. The river's surface looked like pea soup coming to a boil.

From hour to hour the river's sage-green waters, patched with gray shadows, carried us smoothly along through a remarkable landscape. At one place where we stopped to inspect a white cliff, chalk-white boulders as tall as Craig lay heaped at the base like an eerily bleached lava field. Many writers since Meriwether Lewis have compared the eroded bluffs to architecture. As Stanley Vestal said: "Everywhere one sees what appear to be ranges of large free-stone buildings adorned with pale pilasters, long handsome galleries, pinnacles and parapets adorned with statuary, columns with pedestals and capitals entire standing upright or rising pyramidally one above the other until they terminate in a spire or finial."

Our effortless canoeing contrasted sharply with the struggles and tribulations the steamboats had experienced. Their chronicler George Fitch wrote in 1907 that the ideal steamboat for the Missouri "should be hinged in the middle and should be fitted with a suction dredge so that when it cannot climb over a sandbar it can assimilate it.... A steamer that cannot, on occasion, climb a steep clay bank, go across a cornfield and corner a river that is trying to get away, has little excuse for trying to navigate the Missouri."

Black cattle were grazing in head-high grass below a well-known landmark called Hole-in-the-Wall, a gaping wound eroded in a canyon wall. Here Edrie pointed out an area called Johnson Bottom. "This was an especially coveted piece of ground. The first settler filed a claim in 1903, soon after the area was surveyed, but stayed only three and a half years. After him came Jessie Greenwell; she left in 1928. In 1929 John Johnson of Skien, Norway, filed claim here, and he hit upon the right idea for making a go of it. He gave up crops, let the land return to native grasses, and set cattle to grazing on it. That was typical for the modern cattle industry along here."

All week we competed with cattle for campsites. The desirable locations were in the shade of the few groves of cottonwoods, but naturally they were as desirable to the cattle as to us. Even when we shooed them away, evidence of their preference remained. So we sought islands where cattle had seldom ventured.

When we landed on Pablo Island, I walked to the crest of its little hill to look for a good site. I topped it in time to see two does and a fawn swimming the channel toward the opposite shore. Evidently we had frightened them away. They splashed awkwardly through the shallows and bounded up a steep slope. They bounced along stiffly like marionettes yanked from above until they disappeared in the sagebrush. We camped where they had been sleeping, the grasses matted and trampled under the trees, and it was like sleeping in the fingerprint of some great wilderness spirit.

Near the end of our trip we passed Arrow Creek. "Lewis and Clark named it Slaughter River," Edrie said, "for a bison jump a few miles downriver. Indians had driven the bison over a cliff 120 feet high, and the place had 'a most horrid stench.' And the young Swiss artist Karl Bodmer did a painting of these bluffs and the creek in 1833; he put more than 200 Gros Ventre lodges in the scene."

At Lower Rolf Bottom we stopped to see "the most sophisticated ruin on the river," according to Edrie. We beached the canoes under some fine cottonwoods and hiked a mile or so through the knee-high sagebrush. The house stood naked in the baking sun, no shade in sight. Light streamed between horizontal slats in what Sam aptly described as "venetian walls." A rusticated facade of sandstone was mostly gone, but the stone chimney still stood, brave and tall. "Fredrick Rolf homesteaded here in 1909," Edrie said, "but I find no records of him after that. The word 'killed' is supposed to be carved on a rock near here, but I've never been able to find it." Back at the river we rested gratefully in the shade of the cottonwoods before moving on.

On our last day we passed through Deadman Rapids, a riffle now but once — before the days of the dam-builders — a dangerous stretch for canoes. "The name has gone through several variations," Edrie said. "First it was 'Drounded Men,' for some men who traveled from the Judith River to Fort McKenzie in 1837. They went to warn everybody that smallpox had broken out on a boat bringing trade goods. The Blackfeet refused to believe them and demanded that the goods be delivered. On their return trip, a canoe capsized here, and all four men aboard drowned. Their trip was in vain anyway. Smallpox ravaged the Blackfeet camp shortly afterward; it spread until about six thousand people had died of it."

We ended our trip uneventfully at the site of old Camp Cooke. "This was the first Army camp on the upper river," Edrie said. "It was established in 1866. For centuries this had been a favorite campsite for Indians, and many of them came here to harass steamboats. Most Montanans didn't want the Army camp here—they wanted it closer to Helena, because of the government payrolls as well as its protection. It closed in 1870." No sign of it remains today.

The stretch of the Missouri that we canoed was placid and beautiful. Wildlife, of course, was not a threat. We couldn't expect the excitements of Lewis and Clark—a buffalo bull charging past our campfire, a grizzly chasing us into the water, fat wolves proving themselves "extreemly gentle." But we could see the white bluffs that resemble ranges of palaces and galleries, mirrored in delicately shimmering water.

We had hiked to the top of the sculpted bluffs just once, near Eagle Creek, where we were as impressed as Meriwether Lewis had been 170 years before. He wrote in his journal: "I also walked out and ascended the river hills which I found sufficiently fortiegueing. on arriving to the summit . . . I found myself well repaid for my labour. . . ." On the river we had been aware of walls and bluffs beside us, but above them the landscape opened up dramatically. A treeless plain, as flat as Iowa, rolled away to distant mountain ranges in the northwest. The river's course, a gouged canyon, meandered toward the Mississippi. The sun was just setting across the Missouri, and the water glinted silver in the dying light. Montana's big sky enveloped us.

Walking back down a sandy path toward our campsite, Edrie stopped suddenly and pointed. "A tepee ring," she said. There beside us in the grass was a circle of round, unworked stones. Once —who knows why or when—an Indian had put up his traveler's home at this spot. He and his way of life were as vanished now as a steamboat's whistle or an Army bugle's call to arms. As we stood beside the tepee ring in the twilight, the summer air seemed chilly, and we hurried down to our camp.

Weathered antler of a mule deer, shed by spring, lies bleaching in sere grass. "You see antlers at campsites all along the upper Missouri," says Ron. A western species, mule deer range from southern Alaska to the deserts of the Southwest.

At a put-in point on the Missouri, amateur outfitter Craig Lockwood repairs torn canoe canvas with epoxy glue (below) and strips of silver Gaffer-tape (above) applied parallel to the keel. "The patch job worked," he says with satisfaction, "and we didn't take in a drop more for the rest of the trip." At a campsite downstream, he dips up river water — used for dishwashing, but only after boiling. "We had to carry our drinking water in five-gallon containers," says Craig, "because the Missouri's so full of muddy sediment."

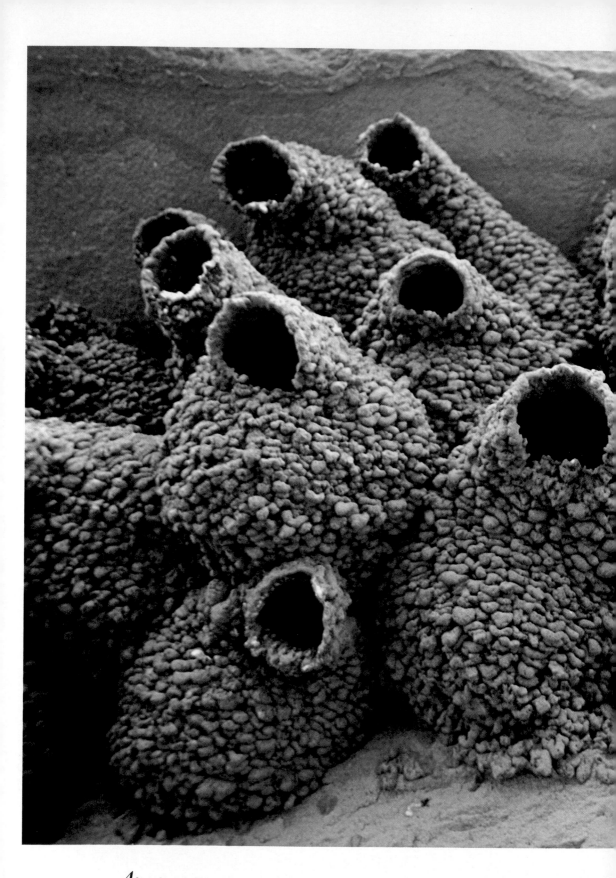

*A*bandoned for winter, clusters of cliff-swallow nests cake the bluffs along the upper Missouri in September. Master masons, these swallows may raise their young in the same nests year after year — or build new structures with gobbets of mud to replace any that have

*crumbled. At a new nest the female lays four or five eggs before she and her mate add
the roof. Before cold weather comes, the flocks have started south on their long migration—
to winter in southern Brazil or central Chile and Argentina.*

Eagle sandstone, a formation conspicuous in the White Cliffs of the Missouri, rises above a jumble of rock in a coulee near the river; the beige and the white surfaces show varying resistance to erosion. Historian Edrie Vinson, who joined Ron and Sam for their Missouri journey, says of this "washed" pattern: "Although there are a few other

examples elsewhere along the river I believe there're none so spectacular."
Whitened bison bones often lie exposed in the cutbanks; these jawbones
and a fragment of shoulder blade had weathered into view at the
site of a prehistoric fire pit. Once, immense herds descended from
the grasslands of the high prairie to drink from the river. In his journal,
Meriwether Lewis noted: "I do not think I exagerate when I
estimate the number of Buffaloe ... at one view to amount to 3000."

Mirrored in the smooth water of the Missouri, natural buttresses of white rock gleam as Edrie Vinson and Ron paddle by. Here, on May 31, 1805, Lewis and Clark and their men came straining upstream towing six canoes and two large pirogues with ropes of hemp or

braided elk leather. That night Lewis wrote: "The hills and river Clifts which we passed today exhibit a most romantic appearance." He compared them to "eligant ranges of lofty freestone buildings, having their parapets well stocked with statuary...."

4

Through Utah's Canyons of Time

I COULDN'T BELIEVE MY EARS. A seemingly rational man had just proposed a scheme that sounded suicidal to me. Mike Hipsher, a young boatman with a Utah outfitter, had contracted to teach me and my companions—Sam, Doug, and Sam's cousin Craig Lockwood—the rudiments of canoeing the Green River's rapids. We stood on its dusty, rocky shore twenty miles above the little town of Green River; before us was Nefertiti Rapid, named for a nearby pinnacle wind-sculpted to resemble the profile of that famous Egyptian queen.

The river narrowed and dropped, creating a classic V in midstream, with standing waves three or four feet high curling back upon themselves. Mike had to shout to make himself heard.

"First," he yelled, "just to get used to the water, we'll go through without the boats." Though obviously this proposal deserved to be hooted down, my companions remained silent and so did I.

Mike distributed life jackets, bulbous orange vests that—though large—seemed barely adequate to me. "Face downstream," he said, "with your feet up in front of you to ward off rocks." Ward off rocks! "Don't try to fight the current—just go with it. When you're through the rapid, let the current carry you to an eddy. Don't try to swim ashore until it does—you'll just wear yourself out." We buckled ourselves into the life jackets, and Mike led us upstream through the tamarisk fifty yards or so above the rapid.

"Everybody ready?" he asked, and I swallowed hard and felt my mouth go dry.

Mike waded out into the stream, and like goslings we followed. The water was cold—its origin had been snow 600 river miles

Black speck on muddy red in the awesome canyonlands of Utah, a powerboat presses upstream on the Colorado River near its junction with the Green. Quiet or rampant, Utah's rivers inspire boatmen with peace and wonder, elation and terror.

WALTER MEAYERS EDWARDS

away in Wyoming's Wind River Range—and the color of coffee with cream. Sparkles from the sun danced and glittered on its surface. I flopped onto my back and began stroking toward the middle of the river. From my vantage point a few inches above the water I could see the white tips of the waves approaching. The roaring grew louder, and I caught a glimpse of the shore rushing past. When I could see the end of unbroken water I got my feet up and I slid— with a sickening lurch, helpless in the grip of the river—down the slope into the rapid. A big wave slugged me in the face and I went under, into a quiet place of hissing green bubbles; I broke the surface, and the roaring and another wave hit me together. I gulped water and went under again, feeling myself bob and spin like a cork.

Quickly it was over. I floated on my back, coughing and sputtering, while the waves diminished, and an eddy caught me and held me. I spotted Sam, grinning at me nearby, and together we worked our way ashore. My shaky knees would barely support me when I regained my feet, elated but tired. The river had scattered us along its banks for about a mile, and when Mike had rounded us up he found us none the worse for our swim.

Later we took the canoes through, and we did a good deal more swimming. We practiced paddling into and out of eddies. This is a tricky business, as currents come at you from two directions and can easily tip a canoe—and did. We practiced swamping a canoe in midstream and righting it by a four-man effort, using a second canoe for leverage. We ran seven rapids that day, and at the end of it we were pretty cocky; we thought we could handle anything we were likely to meet.

Our day of practice with Mike would come in handy later, but for our first trip we picked a gentle and quiet stretch of the river, from the town of Green River 120 miles to the confluence of the Green and the Colorado. We would descend Labyrinth and Stillwater Canyons, and go on into Canyonlands National Park. Our guide and outfitter was Peter Tooker, a lanky young man who had transplanted himself from Washington, D. C. Peter had worked for several years guiding rafting parties through Cataract and Grand Canyons. He brought along a 15-foot inflatable raft that would hold all our provisions and camping gear, leaving the canoes light and maneuverable.

We set off in a drizzle late one morning, and soon the canyon country began to rise before us. We saw it as Frank Leslie described it for his *Illustrated Newspaper* in 1877: "The buttes round Green River are wonderful in size, in shape, and color, and endless inexhaustible variety; there are towers, castles and cathedrals, bulbous knobs and excrescences, colossal mushrooms, 'giant's clubs' and 'giant's teapots,' forts, temples, tombs, and shapes of things, unknown possibly, in the heavens above, and certainly in the earth beneath; all these carved and hewn out of rich red and brown and cream-colored limestone, laid strata upon strata in even bands or stripes of varying color.... The river sweeps in great curves,

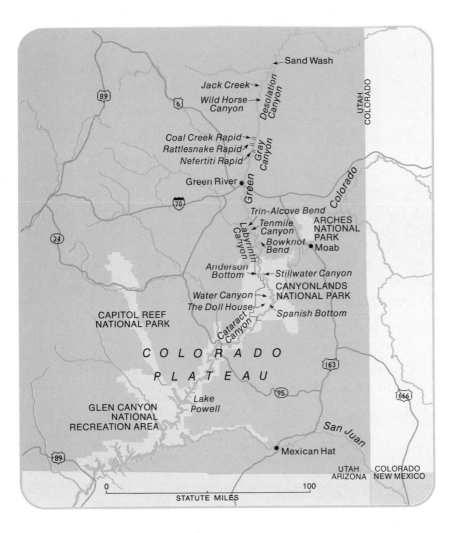

Great rivers dominate the geography of southeastern Utah. Along its canyons the cliffs and buttes, "great mountain masses of rock — are dancing and fading away and reappearing, softly moving about — or so they seem to the eye as seen through the shifting atmosphere." So Maj. John Wesley Powell saw them on the first expedition of record, in 1869. So Ron and his party saw them. They also found, as Powell noted when his small boat swamped, "I see that the place is dangerous." Ron's group made three trips: first on the gentler lower Green to its confluence with the Colorado, then on the more turbulent San Juan, finally on the perilous reaches of the Green through Desolation and Gray Canyons. His party had a notable advantage — they ate better. Powell's men, avid for green stuff, gathered some from a squaw man's bottomland garden. But a diary entry complains, "potato tops are not good greens on the 6th day of July."

washing a white sandy beach with its clear, vivid, emerald-green waters—the brightest, richest green that ever flashed in sunlight, caught from the color of the beds of shale over which it runs."

The current was fast—five miles per hour or so—and roiling. Upwellings from subsurface obstructions broke the surface, sibilant and bubbling. Cliff swallows darted back and forth across the water. The rocky banks were lined with tangled tamarisk bushes in delicate bloom, tiny pale pink flowers among slender feathery leaves. In a stretch of open country an abandoned water wheel lay rusting on the bank. "A rancher installed it to irrigate his fields," Peter said. "But the current cut the bank away, creating an eddy right where he had installed the wheel. It made the current flow upstream instead of down, so the wheel never turned. This river is unpredictable in more ways than one."

Sam picked our campsite that night, and it was the last time we let him do it. We called it our "Guns of Navarone" site for the sandy bluff we had to scale to reach it. Firewood, hauled from an island, stood in for the gear of the saboteurs in the thriller. We had to clamber up the slope with water for cooking, too; but Peter fixed barbecued chicken, soup, green beans, and salad—a far cry from the freeze-dried franks and beans we had so enjoyed in Minnesota.

As in all of our trips, the first day was exhausting. The strain of getting everyone together, of packing up and trying not to forget anything, of being on a new and unfamiliar river, of learning to deal with its special currents and hazards . . . it had worn everyone out, and we were in our tents by 10 p.m.

In the morning, after a sprinkle, it turned hot—and stayed that way. "By July we don't call it Canyonlands," said Peter. "We call it 'Looking for Shade.'" Indeed, shade became a mild obsession for all of us as the daytime temperature stayed around 90°F. We would look for a cottonwood tree or boulder to lunch beside, and before night we tried to find a campsite that would be shaded in the morning. We would hurry to finish breakfast before the sun topped the canyon walls—for cooking over a fire in the blazing sun was torture for Peter, and sizzling bacon loses its allure if you feel you're approaching the sizzling point yourself.

Days we spent drifting with the current, or paddling listlessly.

Botanist and collector, Doug used the brim of his straw hat to dry desert grasses and blossoms—the wild oats shown here as well as peppergrass, prince's plume, and buffalo berry.

We came to call Peter's raft the Tummy Tender; and though I've never been really fond of beer, I found myself paddling up to the raft several times a day for a cold can hoisted dripping from an ice chest. We dipped T-shirts in the river, then put them on. They kept us air-conditioned for an hour or more. Bathing was little help, swimming no fun. With the water at about 60° and the air about 90°, the shock of plunging in took your breath away. Only Sam seemed really to enjoy it.

Side canyons — swaths of tamarisk and cottonwood trees backed by talus slopes and sheer red and gray walls — enticed us off the river a few times. At Tenmile Canyon we paddled up a shallow stream covered with two inches of brown foam like chocolate milkshake. When the stream got too shallow we left the canoes and waded on, the warm mud squishing between our toes. We noticed cat tracks in the warm sand — a big bobcat? a young mountain lion? — and tiny reddish ants working on the face of a hot cliff.

Time was visible on the canyon walls. "The Green River runs through the Colorado Plateau," Peter said. "The entire plain long ago lifted and tilted — say, sixty million years back. Over the eons, the rivers have carved their way through the rock. The farther downriver we go, the older the rocks are alongside us."

Dark stains on the cliff walls, called desert varnish, created bizarre jagged patterns that made me think — ironically — of icicles. In fact they represent the work of water, leaching mineral oxides out of rock and depositing them again as the moisture evaporates.

At Water Canyon we climbed for a mile or so, hiking up terraces like giant stairsteps. We found a streambed with puddles deep enough for bathing — and shallow enough to be warm. We scrubbed and rinsed and splashed, and threw buckets of water on one another. It felt glorious to be clean after days of sand and sweat.

We lunched one day at a spot named by Maj. John Wesley Powell during his expedition down the Green in 1869. "Three side canyons enter at the same point," he wrote. "These canyons are very tortuous, almost closed in from view, and, seen from the opposite side of the river, they appear like three alcoves. We name this Trin-Alcove Bend." Doug wandered up one of the canyons after lunch, and we could hear his clear baritone. "Figaro! Figaro! Figaro!" echoed back and forth in the maze, competing with the calls of the canyon wrens. These little birds sing a series of descending whistles that gradually slow down. They sound exactly as though they're running out of breath. Perhaps they are. On the river, their songs echoed back and forth above us; it reminded me of seeing the Milky Way reflected in the lake in Minnesota.

Cliff swallows often swooped overhead. One morning a score of them launched a mock attack on us, darting back and forth, the rapid *who who who* of their wings the only sound.

Occasionally we came upon Indian sign. A people known as the Anasazi lived along the Green River between A.D. 1000 and 1200. A few of their stone buildings remain, nestled like cliff-swallow nests in nooks and crannies of the canyon walls. Peter took us on several expeditions to visit these little structures, built with slabs laid carefully one atop another. Once we crossed a sere plain covered with sagebrush to a low cliff where four or five of these little buildings remained. Some had hatchways; all were so tiny that I wondered about the size of the Indians who inhabited them—if indeed these were dwellings. Another day Sam and I climbed to the top of a mesa where the Indians had built a tower, probably used as a lookout. It was circular, about 12 feet tall, with small openings where joists had rotted away; we could see the river for miles in either direction. It had been built with mud mortar, now largely weathered out, and the topmost stones had fallen.

At Bowknot Bend we reached another area clearly described by Major Powell: "... we go around a great bend to the right, five miles in length, and come back to a point within a quarter of a mile of where we started. Then we sweep around another great bend to the left, making a circuit of nine miles, and come back to a point within 600 yards of the beginning.... The men call it a 'bowknot' of a river; so we name it Bowknot Bend." We climbed across the "knot"—straight up across the scree, it seemed—and watched as Peter in his raft towed the canoes around the loop. From our height, 500 feet above the river, he looked like a toy man in a toy raft.

One evening, camped near the confluence, we heard a light clattering-and-tinkling across the river and looked up to see desert bighorn sheep coming for a drink: six of them, four ewes and two young. They were coming down a sloping ledge in single file, nearly noiseless in the dusk. Our presence at a fire didn't seem to trouble the ewes; the young ones scampered and kicked with what can only have been glee. At the river they knelt and drank, lifting their heads to peer round them occasionally. After only a few minutes, they started back the way they had come. One of the youngsters gave a bleat and rushed back for one last drink, then hurried to catch up.

And finally we came upon the confluence, where the Colorado River sweeps in from the left. "Late in the afternoon the water becomes swift and our boats make great speed...," wrote Powell. "An hour of this swift running brings us to the junction of the Grand [the Colorado] and Green.... These streams unite in solemn depths, more than 1,200 feet below the general surface of the country." We camped three miles downriver, at a riverside site known as Spanish Bottom, and next day we made the 1,200-foot climb to an area called The Doll House. Here pinnacles eroded by the wind and rain resemble bizarre dolls of every shape and size.

Returning to camp in the evening, as we crossed Spanish Bottom, I nearly stepped on a rattlesnake. Hurrying through the gathering darkness, I heard it *buzzzz* right at my feet. Though it was the first rattlesnake I had ever heard, the sound was unmistakable. (It's a melancholy fact that the snake, being deaf, never hears itself rattle.) Instinctively I danced away from the sound, and then saw the rattler waiting, small and mottled brown, coiled beneath a clump of sagebrush. I walked the rest of the way with my teeth gritted. "A lot of people see them," Peter reassured me, "but I've never heard of anyone on a river trip being bitten."

We stayed at Spanish Bottom for two days, waiting for the large motorboat from Green River that would take us back. Lizards were everywhere: pale brown creatures sunning themselves on rocks, slithering across the sand. One night we hiked half a mile downstream to visit a party of rafters who had passed us, and there on the bank was a sign: STOP — CATARACT CANYON — HAZARDOUS RAPIDS — 200 YARDS AHEAD. We could hear an emphatic warning, a distant, pulsing, stormy roar, and when we could see the rapid I was thankful to be on land. Across the Colorado stretched a bed of ledges and boulders and surging water we could not have survived.

I asked Peter what the fascination was, why people come from all over the country to Utah's dangerous waters. "These rivers provide every emotion," he told me. "Exhilaration, terror, supreme peace. After you've spent some time on them, the wondrous becomes commonplace, and the commonplace becomes wondrous."

The rapids of Cataract Canyon are much too big for open canoes. For our first whitewater run we turned to the San Juan, a river that flows westward across the southeastern corner of Utah and empties into Lake Powell.

We started our trip — with the same crew but different canoes — at the dusty little town of Mexican Hat, named for a rock formation shaped like a sombrero. A string of motels and gas stations, mobile homes and empty corrals, the town slept in the glaring Utah sun. Navajo Indians from the reservation across the river peered at us from their pickups. Sage hens skittered through the brush as we made our way to the bank. The river, a dirty brown, rushed along faster than the Green, with sticks and foam darting past us.

We had tough new whitewater canoes, made from the same nearly indestructible synthetic material as bowling balls. Our wood-and-canvas Old Towns were too fragile for the San Juan's rapids. We also had a Sportyak, a 38-pound, 3½- by 7-foot bathtub-like one-man craft often used on western rivers. Made of plastic, it's virtually unsinkable, and mighty hard to tip over.

Our first day out, Peter stopped us at a point where a huge boulder against one bank created a classic eddy. The water, coming downstream, hit the rock and turned and headed upstream: twin currents, side by side, flowing in opposite directions. Here we practiced canoeing in and out of an eddy. It's the best way to beach a canoe in a fast river, better by far than simply running full tilt against the shore. That afternoon our practice came in handy as we encountered our first rapids.

You hear a rapid coming — like a train — before you see it. You round a bend and the noise is there, a distant rumble. Your heart goes a little faster, your mouth goes dry. You grip your paddle a little harder and brace your knees against (Continued on page 118)

Muscle and paddle fight white water in the San Juan River, formidable tributary of the Colorado. Doug and Ron boss their canoe through a rapid almost as turbulent as an *open boat can run with safety. On a scale of one to six, this rapid approaches three in difficulty;*

beyond that, river runners need inflatable rafts or decked boats. Boulders like those on shore lie on the river bottom; water rushing against them surges up into standing waves, or swirls over them in turbulence that could hold a canoeist under and drown him.

In Stillwater Canyon on the lower Green, Craig and Doug slow their paddles to admire the sandstone spectacle, "a whole land of naked rock," that had impressed Major Powell—"a strange, weird, grand region." Before them, a stand of Fremont poplar and tamarisk marks a likely campsite known as Anderson Bottom. The gigantic boulder at left, split from a cliff in the distant past, carries a sign posted for an annual motorboat cruise sponsored in late spring by Chambers of Commerce in the towns of Moab and Green River.

Year round, the high stone
land lies bare, fringed
with green only at
waterside. In late May,
Encelia frutescens
(right) comes into flower.

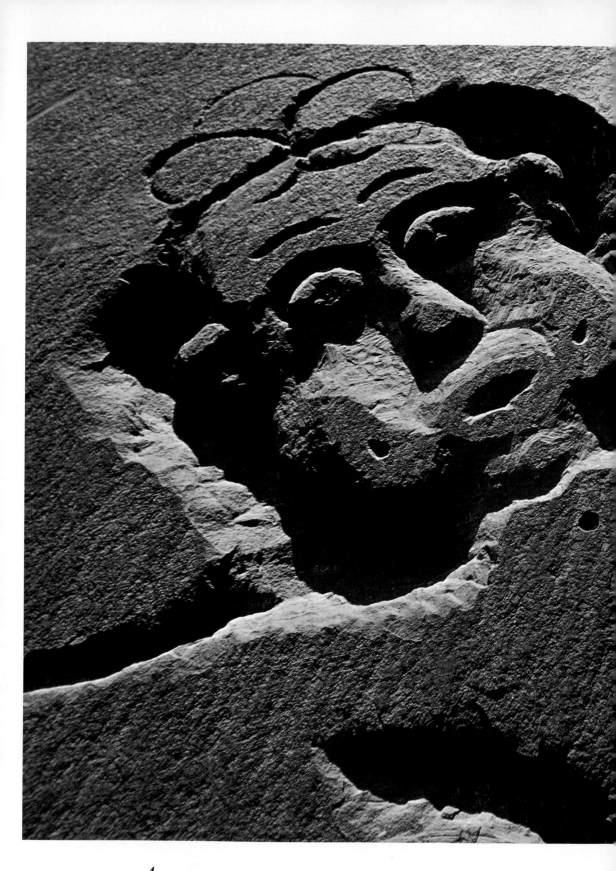

A goggle-eyed figure, larger than life and listing sharply, records a visit to the lower Green by an unknown traveler sometime before World War II. This rough-cut carving dominates a smooth 400-foot billboard of sandstone in Labyrinth Canyon. Since the early

1900's, passersby have stopped and scrambled up the scree to add their names and art to this river register. Ron and his companions lunched here, but chose not to add to the clutter of modern petroglyphs—whose Indian counterparts survive on cliffs upstream and down.

"*B*est stopping place of all," says Sam Abell of this alcove by the San Juan. "We retreated here from a windstorm, relaxed on nice flat rocks, read, and ate good food." Guide Peter Tooker (far left) did all the cooking; Ron especially relished his shrimp supper and fancy breakfasts. Pimiento, green pepper, and onion seasoned his scrambled eggs cooked in a Dutch oven (below). The party's big-rapids expert, Alan Shino, a Japanese-American who teaches the martial arts of the Orient, crouches with supple ease to blow bits of lighted kindling wood into a steady flame.

the sides of the canoe. The roaring grows and the wind picks up—there always seems to be a stiff breeze blowing across rapids.

You slide down the slope of the V and watch your bow partner rise in the air. "Whump!" The bow drops into the trough, water comes at you from every direction, a wave rises beside you like a tsunami. The canoe lurches, tries to turn sideways; your knees slide out from under you. You flail with your paddle, trying to steer, even trying to get your paddle into the bouncing waters. Waves break over the gunwales, and cold water sloshes back and forth around your legs, making a tippy craft even tippier. Then suddenly you're safe and bouncing through the riffles.

About the nicest thing to be said about rapids, I think, is that usually they don't last long. I often thought of a line from an old folk song: "I'm worried now, but I won't be worried long." But as the sound of one faded behind us, we could frequently pick up the murmur of another coming.

During a rest, Peter talked to us about the different kinds of rapids on canyon rivers. "Some are formed by the lay of the land," he said. "If the river is forced through a narrow opening the water has to flow faster to get through. But most of our rapids occur where a side canyon comes in. Spring storms wash boulders down them into the stream. These are called 'boulder gardens.' They're the tricky ones. You have to do some maneuvering."

Classification of the rapids on western rivers differs from the system used by the American Whitewater Affiliation. "Out here, where we do mostly rafting and kayaking, they're usually rated on a scale of one to ten," Peter told us. "That started after World War II, with Otis Marston, an early river runner. When someone asked him how tough a particular rapid was, he'd say, 'Well, on a scale of one to ten. . . .' So the system grew up from that. Generally, class I is a riffle, class V or VI is about the limit for open canoes, and class X is all but unmanageable, even in a big pontoon raft."

With the rapids keeping us busy, it was easy to miss the spectacular countryside. Canyon walls—patterned by strata of brown and green and rust—rose beside us, often from the very edge of the river. Years of moviegoing had conditioned all of us to look for a string of warbonneted Indians silhouetted against the sky.

At night we slept on open sleeping bags, warmed by the heated sand beneath us and the hot summer breezes. Overhead the moon, a few days short of full, cast a light nearly strong enough to read by, and the Big Dipper did its stately, wheeling waltz. Canyon walls turned gray in the moonlight.

I looked forward to the campsites at the end of the stress-filled days. I would find myself a comfortable spot, lean back against a canoe, perhaps with a plastic cup of chilled white wine, jot down notes, sniff the soup cooking—Peter "urging forward the supper"—and watch the sun set behind one butte while an early moon rose above another. At such times the river gurgling beside me finally seemed like a friend, another member of our party.

Peter, a marvel of efficiency and good humor, kept us well fed and happy. And amused. He wore a small silver medallion around his neck, and when he leaned over the fire it often dangled close to the flames. When he straightened up, the hot medallion landed on his naked chest and made him yelp like a puppy. Thanks to Peter, my idea of roughing it now includes a supper of shrimp, fried rice, a fresh spinach-and-mushroom salad, apple pie with coffee — and a breakfast of French toast and bacon. Somehow, in the broiling desert, Peter managed to end a six-day trip with ice left over.

A big wind nearly blew us off the river as we approached Lake Powell. Tumbleweeds the size of beach balls dashed and jostled along the banks and dropped into the river. Broadside gusts sent the canoes veering from bank to bank in spite of our strongest efforts. Going through a small rapid in the midst of the storm I lost a hat. It whirled through the air like a Frisbee and quickly sank. Clouds of sand swirled around us, stinging and filling our eyes with grit.

"Pull over under that ledge," shouted Peter. We beached the boats near a massive overhang and huddled under it while the storm blew. The sky turned gray behind the clouds of blowing sand, and the sun was just a pale dish.

Snug and comfortable out of the wind, we camped there even though it was early in the day. The only bad thing about the site was its floor. Around useful flat rocks to sit on, there were several inches of very fine soil. "This is silt from Lake Powell," Peter explained. "The lake reaches its greatest depth at the end of the summer, and this place is under water. During the winter the lake falls because of the continued use of water for hydroelectric power." I've never felt grubbier than I did in the morning, after sleeping in a bed of dust that vagrant gusts would sift onto me.

Next day the river gradually turned into lake; the current slowed, then stopped, and the water reached into side canyons. We waded up a couple of them, the water only a few inches deep over the silt.

During the long drive back to Green River, Peter — beside me in the jeep — dozed off. After a while he woke up, looked around, and smiled. "I had a funny dream," he said. "I dreamed I was clean."

Our last trip in Utah taught us an impressive reality. Wallace Stegner had defined it in 1954, in *Beyond the Hundredth Meridian*: "... what every man who has ever handled a boat on Green or Colorado or San Juan learns: how trivial a mistake can lead to trouble. The rivers are not 'treacherous.' They are only forever dangerous. One who has not tried it finds it hard to believe the instant and terrible force that such a current exerts...."

We had plenty of opportunities to assess this "instant and terrible force" during a 96-mile journey down the Green from Sand Wash to the town of Green River. About 80 riffles and rapids — some of them far larger than anything we had yet experienced — were scattered through Desolation and Gray Canyons.

With us was Alan Shino, a young Japanese-American. (His

*Bighorn sheep—four ewes and two young—
drink from the Green in deepening twilight,
apparently untroubled by the presence of
the canoeists, fifty yards away across the
river. "They came down a ledge rather
slowly," Ron remembers. "From the moment
we noticed them it took them about ten
minutes to reach the river's edge.
But they didn't seem bothered by our fire;
they drank quite calmly. We all sat
as still as we could, and nobody said
anything as long as we had them in sight."*

father had lived in Hawaii before Alan was born and, while working on a mountaintop one Sunday morning in 1941, had a ringside
seat for the attack on Pearl Harbor.) A student of chemical engineering, Alan teaches kayaking at the University of Utah. He also gives
demonstrations of the martial arts of the Orient. He could make a
whitewater canoe do everything but dance, and it was a joy to see
him in action. "Alan's as good at canoeing as I've ever seen anybody
good at *anything*," Sam would say later.

It was even hotter on this trip, for we were deep into June.
Sunglasses and long-billed caps did little to deflect the blinding
glare on the water. "Remember how in Maine we sought out the
sun?" Sam reminded me. "How we looked for sunny beaches for
lunch stops? It would be nice to have some of that weather here
now." There was little incentive to sleep late in the mornings. When
the sun hit the sleeping bags, it popped us out like pieces of toast.

Thunderous rapids waited for us around bend after bend in
Desolation Canyon. At Jack Creek, Alan and I practiced ferrying, a
technique for getting from one bank to the other in a rapid. As we
stood knee-deep near shore, holding the canoe, Alan explained the
method. "We'll keep the canoe headed upstream, at about a 45-
degree angle to the current. I'll steer; you paddle just hard enough
to maintain our position. The river will carry us across." It seemed

to me another of those schemes likely to drown me, and I said so.

"Why not just go downstream a ways and paddle across?"

Alan just laughed. "Get in the canoe."

Improbably, it worked. The force of the current against the angled bow pushed us straight across the river, the canoe bucking and lurching like a bronco.

Alan pointed out some of the hazards lurking in big rapids. "A boulder in midstream with water flowing over it is called a 'pillow.' From upstream, pillows appear as just smooth humps in the river. Some of them—big ones—are called 'keepers,' because if you go over them, the turbulence on the other side will hold you there, on the bottom. Stay away from them."

Because rapids are so deceptively placid seen from upstream, we followed sound procedure—stop before each one, walk down to it and look it over, plot the best route through. That was usually the most frightening part of the run, since the anticipation of terror exceeds the actual fright. I would find myself standing on a slippery boulder while at my feet the river went mad—tons of water driven berserk by boulders, a chaos of thunder and wildness. Is that me trembling, I wondered, or is it the rock underfoot? V's as smooth as oil led straight into pandemonium, an impossible tangle of waves and stone. And the pulsating roar never stopped.

Our third day out we ran 18 rapids. We nearly swamped at every one, with speeds up to 25 miles an hour. Usually Peter went first in his raft, swooping and dancing, the raft sometimes folding nearly double. Then he would rest his oars and wait. It was a reassuring sight to see him in the distance, ready to pick us up if we spilled.

That day the incident occurred that came to be called Ron's Big Swim. Sam and Doug had stopped on shore; Peter for once was bringing up the rear. I was in the bow of Alan's canoe as we approached a rapid above Wild Horse Canyon. It looked neither bigger nor more difficult than many we had run without trouble, and as I braced myself and gripped my paddle I expected no trouble here. We slid down the V into the first wave and immediately it landed in my lap. Another one followed, and another, and before we were halfway through we were swamped, up to our waists in the river. The canoe was floating—but underwater.

"Better get out," Alan shouted above the tumult, and we swung easily out of the canoe. It bobbed to the surface upside down. We hung on to it in water too deep for any kind of footing.

"Work your way back here," he yelled, and I pulled myself along the hull to the stern. We both got hold of the stern line and tried to work the canoe toward shore, but a swamped canoe seems to weigh a ton. Now Craig came down in the Sportyak; Alan grabbed the back of it while Craig rowed toward shore. But the strain was too much. Alan kept his grip on the Sportyak, but the canoe's line slipped from his grasp. In an instant the Sportyak was 20 yards away. The current picked up speed and I looked downstream. And my heart lurched into my throat: another rapid, a big one. I could see its plumes of white dancing above its lip; Alan and Craig were barely in sight beyond them. I let go of the canoe as it rushed toward the rapid.

"I'm too close to shore," I thought. "There are boulders along here." I got myself into position, feet up, trying to remember everything Mike had taught us, just as I slid down the edge of the V.

Water exploded over me, hissing and bubbling. I came up, gulped a mouthful of water, and dropped over a pillow. Its maelstrom toppled and twisted me. Another wave broke in my face, and I caught a glimpse of a large smooth hump in my path—another pillow. My feet caught briefly against it and the current hurled me forward over it in a flailing topsy-turvy somersault. I felt my knees scrape across the rock. It seemed a long time before I came up.

But that big one wasn't a keeper. The current washed me into an eddy and then against the shore. I scrambled up onto a dry boulder, my teeth chattering and knees wobbling. Soon Peter came down in the raft—*"You all right?"* He took me on to a sandbar where we found Alan and Craig, and the lost canoe. As we regrouped, the others lavished sympathy and care on me. Shaking uncontrollably, I accepted wool sweaters and a cup of hot tea—Peter had a fire going in minutes. He gave me some ice for a bloody knee.

Damage to the canoe was more serious. Its splashguard was

gone; a crack gaped at the bow. Peter and Alan patched it up with a nail-studded piece of driftwood they found, and on we went.

Thereafter I never stopped being impressed by the speed and force of the river. The next day I spent rowing the raft, a ponderous tub of a thing, with oars that weighed 20 pounds apiece. You row facing downstream in the rapids, the better to see your route. Instead of smashing into waves like a canoe, the raft followed their contour, giving an exhilarating roller-coaster ride.

Then I tried the Sportyak. It's agile, but as in all rowboats you can get mixed up and pull on the wrong oar at crucial moments. I nearly smashed into a jagged rock wall in Rattlesnake Rapid, then missed an enormous pillow by inches. Its thunderous cascade swept by right at my elbow.

On our last day I went back to canoeing. Paddling along, I would see an obstacle a hundred yards away. By the time I thought "I must do something to avoid that," I would be right on top of it, digging furiously in a last-ditch effort to escape destruction. Alan's reactions, in contrast, were instantaneous and powerfully effective. Once, as we ran a rapid with me again in the bow, a small pillow appeared directly in front of us. I froze, abandoned hope, and readied myself for another swim. With one sweeping backstroke Alan stopped us, turned the canoe, and guided us past the boulder, backward! With another stroke he turned us again, and off we went. I looked back to see him grinning at me.

"Close one," he said.

And then the Green turned us loose. It's a river full of excitement — almost too much. We got an expert, and gratifying, verdict on our trip when we turned in our raft and rented gear back at the outfitter's at Green River. Four boatmen were there, burly young fellows in shorts and sandals. They were checking the provisions and raft and life jackets they would use the next weekend. I heard one of them questioning Craig: "Where've you guys been?"

"On the Green."

"In open canoes?"

"Yeah. Sure."

"Heyyyyy — a bunch of hot dogs!"

As for me, I looked forward to the placid waters of Yellowstone Lake.

Bouncy as beach balls, scratchy tumbleweeds scatter their seed for mile after mile as they roll in desert winds. Many of them grow from a small tangle of stems to bushel-basket size.

Carved by wind and rain, a few grains of sand at a time, the russet stonescapes in Arches National Park hold forms like urns and olive jars, finials and fingertips. Such shapes express the composition of the rock; softer, more friable surfaces erode to leave the smaller, more

tightly cemented grains. In cracks of a gnarled monolith, scrubby piñon trees send their roots wide for moisture—and stability in the desert winds. To visit the park, Ron and his party made a 35-mile side trip from the little town of Green River southeast by road toward the Colorado. 125

Off-river sight-seeing: In a creek canyon near the lower Green, Peter and Doug's lead canoe slashes a foam like chocolate milkshake. Whipped up when brief waterfalls tumbled over canyon rims during a hard rain, the froth curdled with fine silt and floated downstream. "Fun to play in," says Sam. On the Green, spotting Indian ruins on high ledges became a counting game. The tiny rooms at right, probably used by the Anasazi to store corn and other crops, have lasted some

800 years; chinking of mud made them rodent-proof. Just beyond the Green's entrance into the Colorado, Doug and Craig climbed 1,200 feet through crevices to see pinnacles shaped like gigantic kachina dolls.

Beginning a day of shooting 25 rapids on the Green, Alan and Doug lay out their route through a stretch of white water. "It always sounds terrifying," recalls Sam. "Scarier than doing the run itself." To photograph an expert in extreme conditions, Sam rode backward in the bow to face Alan as sternman. Bow first, the canoe rose like a roller-coaster car to a wave's crest. Then the canoe dipped abruptly and dropped, jerking the stern—and Alan—into the air (below). With Sam handling a camera instead of a paddle, the canoe wrested control from Alan. Waves whipped in. The boat sank. Sam made it to shore with his camera safe; Alan saved the canoe. Generally, river thrills

exceed the frights. Each season, sports lovers by the hundred ride kayaks in the rapids of Utah's rivers; about a score take on big rapids in canoes. Thousands pay to jounce through on safer rafts that buck like broncos.

In a swamping recorded by Craig, the San Juan spills Sam and Doug. As the canoe capsizes, they flail and fall and roll out. Holding splashguards and ropes at bow and stern, they made shore a mile downstream. Ron's "Big Swim" came in the Green River. After swinging from a wave-filled canoe, Alan gripped the

stern of a rescue craft. But Ron, swept away by the roaring water, tumbled over boulders until an eddy saved him. Soon Peter, in a raft, picked him up. Above, chilled to the bone, he holds ice to a bloody knee. He still calls this experience "easily the most frightening moment of my life."

*Desert varnish—dark streaks of iron and other oxides—patterns a canyon wall above
the Green River. Ron and Doug, with a load of tumbleweed collected along the way, pause to
study the coloring brought out by a rain shower just ended. On dry rock the stains may show less*

*contrast, less luster. Over the centuries rain leaches the minerals out of stone, only to
deposit them again as the rivulets of runoff evaporate on the rock face. The curving
strata of crossbedded sandstone in this cliff record sand dunes older than 125 million years.* 133

5

Canoes and Camps in the Rockies

JOHN COLTER WAS ALONE in the Rockies, trudging through country never before seen by a white man. With a 30-pound pack, a pair of snowshoes, and vague directions gleaned from Indians, he spent many months exploring the area later made famous by Yellowstone National Park. At home in the wilderness, Colter had left the Lewis and Clark Corps of Discovery on August 17, 1806, to join up with some trappers; now he searched for fresh beaver country.

Nearly three decades after Colter's lonely trek, Washington Irving described it in *The Rocky Mountains*, imagining the "gloomy terrors" Colter had witnessed: "hidden fires, smoking pits, noxious streams, and the all-pervading 'smell of brimstone.'" About 170 years after Colter's adventure, we camped on the shore of Yellowstone Lake, almost in the shadow of a peak named in his honor.

As the summer turned toward fall once more, Sam and I felt we had had a temporary surfeit of canoe camping, the wearying, point-to-point trips that demand a prescribed number of miles a day. With sunset coming a little earlier every day, it became harder and harder to find campsites before dark. And if you've ever tried pitching a tent or fixing supper or taking a bath in the dark, you understand the importance of camping before nightfall. Even finding sugar for your tea is more trouble than it's worth when you know you have to rummage through a bulging Duluth pack in the dark to find it — probably spilled, or wet, or missing.

"Has anybody seen the honey?"

"Who's got the salt?"

"Somebody hand me a fork, please."

Songs of the wilderness, we came to call such refrains.

Free from summertime crowds, Wyoming's Jackson Lake gives Craig Lockwood a welcome solitude. Behind him on the eastern shore lies Signal Mountain Lodge; peaks of the Tetons rise beyond. Ron and his party went to the Rockies for camping and canoeing in late autumn.

Add a little cold or rain to the darkness, and misery and gloom settle onto a camp like a fog.

This trip would be different, we decided. We would canoe slowly down Yellowstone Lake, camping along the way. Sam, Craig, and I were joined by Terry Hunt, a friend of Sam's from Washington. Good-natured and witty, Terry had done little canoeing or camping, so we looked forward to teaching him the ropes.

The Rocky Mountains rose around us as we drove through the park toward our put-in point on the lake. A young coyote, chasing a mouse in a meadow alongside the road, bounced stiff-legged like a puppy through the tall grass. A massive black buffalo stood grazing, ignoring the line of camera-clicking tourists parked along the road.

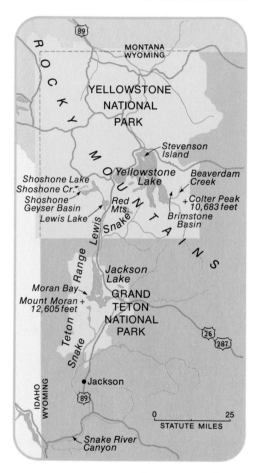

We made our latest start ever, launching the canoes well after six o'clock in the afternoon. But the lake was serene, and the evening light, soft and warm.

We had paddled barely an hour when the wind drove us ashore on a rocky beach. Later we learned more about this afternoon phenomenon: The air above the lake, warmed by the sun, rises and creates thunderstorms; as the sun declines, the air cools and descends onto the lake, creating strong and gusty winds that whip the water into frothing whitecaps.

Sam and I sat up late, talking and watching the moon—about half full—set in the lake. It seemed to roll over onto its back and turn yellow as it approached the horizon, then flatten and sink to just a pinpoint of light over the water. Finally, it twinkled like a star and flickered out.

Next morning there was frost twinkling on the canoes and tents, an eighth of an inch of ice in the water bucket. But the day warmed quickly, and the canoes made paths through acres of yellow algae that blanketed the clear water. A loon bobbing like a decoy had its wild song perfectly timed to its echo: An identical interval lapsed between its call, the echo, and the next call.

Again that afternoon the wind drove us ashore, depositing us at a campsite south of Park Point on an arm of the lake where motorboats are prohibited. We set up the tents, fluffed the sleeping bags, changed into warm dry clothes, and gave Terry a cooking lesson. We buried a roast, potatoes, and onions, all wrapped in foil, in hot coals near the fire. Before long, we could hear them sizzling. Craig fixed cheesecake for dessert, and we felt we'd done ourselves proud.

Headwaters of the Snake in Yellowstone Park, where rules permit no boats on any creek, drain toward Grand Teton National Park, where hand-propelled craft may explore creeks or lakes—weather permitting.

"Wait till you've tried my pancakes," Terry boasted. "This supper will pale to nothing by comparison."

In the morning Terry indeed made pancakes, but most of them ended up in the gullet of a panhandling California gull. "They taste fine to me," said Terry. We suggested that he had practiced on us and served himself last, after he had got the hang of it.

"One of these days, lentil soup," he warned. "You won't *believe* my lentil soup."

We caught a few fish—cutthroat trout—but couldn't keep any. Park rules for Yellowstone Lake allow you to keep only fish less than 13 inches long, a reversal of most fishing regulations. Ordinarily you keep the big ones, throw back the little ones. But, for a variety of ecological reasons, mature fish are protected here.

A hiking trail ran through the woods behind our campsite; and when the incessant, thumping surf got on our nerves, we would stroll through the somber forest. One afternoon, when the wind had kept us trapped at the same site for several days, I walked down the beach a mile or so, toward a flock of waddling geese that nonchalantly took to the water as I approached. Then I cut off into the woods and into the silence. High above, the tips of the pines nodded in a breeze, but no sound reached me. Shafts of sunlight, flecked with dust motes, dappled the moist floor.

Terry had set his lentils to soak overnight, and he fretted and fussed like a French chef over the pot as the soup simmered that afternoon. But somewhere he had miscalculated.

"Someone pass the salt, please."

"Sorry, it's all in the soup."

The cook, at least, is spared the clean-up chores. I came to dread a nightly ritual on all our trips: washing the dishes. I would find myself squatting in the mud over a bucket of icy river or lake water, a plastic flashlight clenched in my teeth, scrubbing burnt macaroni out of a blackened pot—my hands freezing, my creaky knees screaming for relief, water slowly seeping into my boots.

But it was good to be camped in one spot. Point-to-point canoe trips can be exhausting. It's a little like moving your household every day: tearing down your home in the morning, packing up, moving on, building a new home every night, all the while keeping your family warm and fed and sheltered.

An enormous wind rocked our tents that night, the flaps cracking, the lines humming like flutes, and the waves sounding very close as they crashed onto the beach. In the morning the wind continued strong—too strong for canoeing, though we were due to leave. We waited through that day and the next, but still it howled, spitting snow. So Craig and I hiked 12 miles to the car—through the dark, snow-spotted forest, with shy deer peering at us from thickets, their tails flicking nervously—and the rangers' patrol boat made an emergency pickup for Sam and Terry and the cargo.

Then, unfortunately, I had to leave the Rockies; and so we've arranged to have Sam pick up the story. *(Continued on page 144)*

*I*ndian summer brings a crew in shirtsleeves to begin a trip on Yellowstone Lake: Terry Hunt, who sizes up the gear to be loaded, Craig, and Ron in his long-billed antisunburn cap. Behind Craig, five miles of placid water stretch toward Stevenson Island. The

course: south. Superb visibility and a rare afternoon calm marked the launching for a trip on the largest high-mountain lake in the 48 States. Covering 139 square miles, it rests at an elevation of 7,733 feet. Its fall moods quickly become clear—in abrupt changes.

Wet snow and shut-in conditions idle the canoes the first morning out. In bad weather the group stayed ashore; as visibility improved, they scouted the area. At right, Sam and Terry check a route against a map. They backpacked to Brimstone Basin, a geyser region dormant in historic times. Hiking along Beaverdam Creek, they found the unspoiled wilderness of Yellowstone. The park holds the largest concentration of thermal features — geysers, hot springs, fumaroles, sulphur pools — in the world. "Water-That-Keeps-On-Coming-Out," Indians called the geyser basins. Some tribes feared them as the abode of

evil spirits; others hunted animals that gathered there for warmth in cold seasons. In 1870 an inept explorer, lost in a bitter storm, survived by sleeping on hot ground and boiling elk-thistle roots in a hot spring; he lost half his weight, and scalded his hands—but he lived to be rescued.

CRAIG LOCKWOOD

Evening winds, damp and cold, lash a camp at Yellowstone Lake. Craig, warily warming his hands, watches the fire consume wood at a ferocious rate and wonders how soon it will burn down to a bed of coals suitable for cooking. "It's tricky to cook in gusty wind," observes Ron; "wind whips the heat away, and you have to set the pots closer to the coals. Sometimes we cheated with the coffeepot and put it right in the flames." In spite of wind, says Terry, "it was fun cooking my favorite recipes outdoors, and everything tasted so good. I even learned a recipe from Sam and Ron, for scrambled eggs with cheese and scallions." Fortunately, the party found a plentiful supply of driftwood scattered along the lakeshore; a small pond behind base camp cradled a weathered, wind-felled tree.

SEVERAL DAYS PASSED AFTER RON LEFT before Craig and Terry and I were canoeing again. Those days took the snow with them, and now we stood on the bank of the Snake River, ready to start south to Jackson Lake. We had a well-informed guide named Ed Riddell, a seasonal employee of the Park Service, and a short stretch of river ahead. The only reminder of that sudden storm was our breath, which formed small cumulus clouds in the cold, brilliantly bright dawn air.

Between bursts of breath and steaming sweat as we loaded the canoes, we could sense a fine autumn day beginning. The Snake flowed quietly, so shallow that Ed wasn't positive our canoes would make it through. With a gentle pivot we swung into the current. Now, on the right river almost all the work is done — it's a matter of simple steering, and seeing the world slide slowly past. On this unfolding day we had the right river and a world worth seeing.

On the banks, aspen trees were points of white and gold in a dark mural of rolling conifer green. Above all this, expansive and proud as the national anthem, were the tops of the Tetons. By now these must surely be the popular image of mountains, so classical is their granite-and-snow shape. It was as though we were paddling into a calendar and about to become the picture for October.

Over the riffles, rising mist made the river seem out of breath as we drifted downstream, just clearing the rocky bottom. An eagle was ahead of us, alternately flying and perching high in riverside pines. Finally it wheeled wide of the Snake and soared away.

We ate lunch where the Snake flows into Jackson Lake, a natural lake dammed to raise its level. In autumn, when the water level is down, remnants of the old forested shoreline — stumps and trunks — protrude from the water. We canoed in the channel of the old river, with the "new" shallow lake on either side. Our route held along the western shore, the wilderness side of Jackson Lake, where no roads or campgrounds exist. It's easily accessible only by boat, but even boating parties tend to go elsewhere.

We soon came upon an area where a forest fire had burned. Charred and blackened trees, some fallen and some still standing, evoked a no-man's-land of World War I. But a new generation of greenery, seedlings and little bushes, was working to establish itself. The Park Service, under a policy adopted in 1974, had not attempted to put the fire out, but had let it run its course. Ed explained why.

"Basically," he said, "Grand Teton Park's divided into three management zones. In zone one we usually let natural fires burn. Zone two is a decision-making zone: A committee orders the fire controlled if it's likely to spread to areas that are populated or developed. In zone three all fires are put out, natural or man-made.

"This fire was started by lightning in early July 1974. It just smoldered for approximately two months, and consumed five acres. But that was a dry summer and a very dry September, and the fire took off and ended up burning about 3,500 acres.

"Someday, this area will be healthier than it was before. We've

Ringed with stones gathered at leisure, a camp hearth warms food and coffee. Once Ron's party heaped coals over the Dutch oven to bake brownies; within 30 minutes the batter burned to cinders.

been doing intensive biological studies here, and we can tell that recently burned areas are supporting more wildlife than the others. That's simply because there's more understory. In an old forest it's all pine needles. By the way, lodgepole pine—the dominant species here—is fire-dependent. Certain of its cones are designed to open and drop seeds during a fire. It has evolved with fire. Needs it."

Our first campsite was uneventful until night: As day's light and sound faded and fell to nothing, they were replaced by a moonless starscape and a primal, haunting sound. In the black forest behind us, elk began bugling. Terry, Craig, and I listened to a sound none of us had heard before. It reminded me of the recorded "songs" of humpback whales: a high-pitched whistling and barking—lyrical, musical, urgent. I thought of Ron, and night in the Okefenokee. Music meant much to him, and he heard more of it in nature than anyone else I've ever camped with. We wished he were here listening with us to this sound-filled quiet.

Elk bugle in several tones and for a variety of reasons, but you only hear them in the fall, the season of the rut, when the bulls have shed the velvet from their antlers by rubbing them on trees. A mixture of bark, sap, dirt, and mud stains the antlers dark brown, almost black. The necks of the males swell enormously, the better to impress the females, and bulls spar with each other in efforts at intimidation. Serious fights are rare. In the late autumn successful bulls patrol the fringes of their harems, bugling possessively.

We set out early and made our way along the lake, still on the western side and passing the burned-over area. About 11 o'clock we stopped and made a hike, over and across the burn and up and down, stopping often, at Terry's request, to "catch the scenery."

Ed pointed to a goshawk wheeling overhead. "There's more evidence the fire was not a bad thing," he said. "If this were still forest you might not see him. Now small animals have moved into the new growth, and goshawks have come to prey on them."

We continued our hike to a remote cabin tucked at the confluence of two small streams.

"It probably belonged to a tusker," Ed said. "Back in the early 1900's there was a real market for elk tusks; people were wearing them on pendants and things like that. The tuskers killed many elk illegally—shoot the creature, remove the tusks, and just leave the carcass. They had cabins back in the woods—away from the law—and some of them haven't been found until recently."

We panted our way back to the canoes and had lunch on a gravel bar. Ours were the only boats in sight, with these towering mountains around us, and we were radiantly happy.

After lunch we approached the lake's islands, interesting but little-known dots of land. Though they are beautifully and naturally landscaped, with meadows and aspens and lodgepole pines, visitors generally pass them by. Then we rounded a point into Moran Bay and at once met the down-canyon winds: a feature of late afternoon, as on Yellowstone. We went from calmness into whitecaps almost immediately. We beat along into the wind until we came to a small bay where a cow moose and an enormous bull were standing. We tried to draw close, but the cow noticed us. Slowly and majestically she left the knee-deep water; she retreated onto a gravel bar, and then into the woods. The male, 50 yards away, did the same. We followed them cautiously into the woods for a while, but only saw them briefly and heard them crashing through the brush—a formidable breaking and thumping sound.

That night we camped at the very head of Moran Bay. Mount Moran, in my opinion the most imposing single peak in the Tetons, towered over us, catching the last light.

"In 1950 a plane carrying 18 missionaries crashed into Mount Moran," Ed told us. "It was in November, and evening, and it seems the pilot flew right into the mountain—probably couldn't even see it. It was 13 days before anybody could even get up to the site, because conditions were so bad. From across the lake you can see the wreckage to this day, when the sun glints off the metal."

The following morning we threaded our way among the islands. The canoeing was serene: calm, glassy water; blue skies. Sun lotion was passed fore to aft on paddle blades.

We lunched on Dollar Island, so named, apparently, because it reminded old-timers of a coin. It was cobbled with white stones that had been covered by lake water earlier in the year. The water left a white coat of dust on the rocks. The shore looked like a beach of eggs, and our instinct was to tread softly on them.

For our last canoeing trip in the Rockies, Craig and I enlisted the help of A. J. DeRosa and Phil Steck, fishing and float-trip guides from Jackson, Wyoming. In the winter both are ski patrolmen in the Tetons. Both love what they do: love to float rivers, love to fish, love to ski. We were in good hands. We planned to canoe across Lewis Lake, up the Lewis River channel, and across Shoshone Lake to the Shoshone Geyser Basin, all within Yellowstone Park.

We took off with snow on the ground and the threat of more in the air. We were nearly the last visitors around. With the first big snowfall after October 31, the park "officially closes." If we saw a storm approach, we would have to make a furious retreat to our car.

The compensations were obvious, though. Again we were on a large lake in a popular park, and we were alone. Ahead, a thermal feature puffed an exclamation point ten feet high above the shoreline. The canoeing came easily; there was time to look around, and all around was serene. Then Lewis Lake gave way to the Lewis River channel, and for the first time we were doing a whole stretch of river in a different direction. Upstream.

Smooth current sped past the canoe and pushed the paddles backward easily. This produced a novel and utterly false sense of speed one doesn't feel going downstream. Craig and I reckoned our progress was cut by at least half. We bent to the paddling: no more drifting and dreaming.

There were occasional wide, slower-moving sections of river. At one, known as The Pool, a large, bright-blue kingfisher dropped from the top of a dead lodgepole pine. It flew directly away from us, just inches above the dark water. As it searched for food it would touch the water and make a bright and instant point of light.

The next birds we encountered flew straight at us. Gorbies! (Canada jays around here.) As usual these friendly fellows were hungry. They flew midstream, stalling and chattering overhead, deftly accepting handouts of crackers, then retreating. The chance of sharing lunch attracted four of them. Politely they took turns.

By now the current was too swift for paddling. We pulled on our hip waders and lined the canoes upstream. Through the cold water the landscape of the river bottom was clearly visible.

It was more than that to A. J. and Phil. Like our guide on the Buffalo River, they could "read" the bottom, and where Craig and I saw only colorful patterns of gravel, they saw "sign" of fish. A. J. showed us shallow bowls of gravel, the size of pie pans. These were "redds"—the spawning beds of brown trout. Schools of brownies, as many as 30 at a time, darted in dark formation inches from our feet. When I spoke optimistically of catching them, Phil told me to forget it: "They just aren't hungry this time of year. Luck out and catch one, and you'll find an empty stomach when you gut him."

Our first camp on Shoshone Lake was near the head of the river. Half a mile away, a group of fishermen from Colorado Springs had camped. They had been coming here for eleven years. Our only conversation with them didn't encourage us about the weather: "A year ago this week there was a snowstorm. Forty-inch drifts."

That day we canoed the length of the lake to a place pleasantly called The Point, a high peninsula pointing south. For three days it was our base camp. We hurriedly set up tents, fluffed out sleeping bags, gathered firewood and water. There was still light enough for a visit to the main attraction: Shoshone Geyser Basin.

Free of cargo, our canoes shot across the shallow little bay. We beached them and walked toward a low hill, adding our lug-soled footprints to the hooves, paws, and claws of elk, moose, coyotes, and grizzly bears. A faint path ran up the hill. We followed it to the rim, and stopped there, dazzled. Columns of mist rose from the fumaroles and hot pots and geysers and thermal pools. The scene was backlighted, which heightened the sense of steamy mystery that always haunts a geyser basin.

Within a rim of dark hills, everything seemed white: a pale, grayish white for the sky; a shadowed white for the snow; the bright mist; the fluid mercury of light on the running water. A seductive breath of warmth from the geysers reached us.

For an hour, wandering about separately, the four of us went exploring. Finally, with too much to see and too little light to see by, we met again at the far end of the valley, where Shoshone Creek enters the lake. It was a calm evening, perfectly tranquil. We stood in cold boots and watched the pinks give way to the blues, which gave way to the darker blues of near night. The first planet rose in the east—clear, perfectly reflected in the marshy bays and still waters of the western rim of the lake. The earth was turning toward night, and we canoed home in the dark.

It was Halloween. Around the campfire, tired storytellers told ghost stories to tired listeners. We turned in early, paying little heed to the scurrying mouse we heard in the cellophane and brown-paper wrappings of our candy supply.

Next morning, up alone and getting ready for a solo trip to the geyser basin, I reached for the drinking water. My hand snapped back: The mouse, frozen, lay in the bucket. Looking for a drop of water, he had slipped in and drowned.

I was drawn to the geyser basin at dawn by the prospect of unusual lighting conditions. At first I saw nothing out of the ordinary. Fog filled the basin. Then the sun rose. Its warmth lifted the white blanket from the valley floor. Gold light poured into the steaming basin, mingling with the silver mist in an unforgettable transformation of night to day.

The others joined me to spend the day wandering about the rim, inhaling the sulphurous smells, admiring the unusual mineral features, taking photographs, and considering the chance of a hot bath. The sport of "hot potting"—bathing in a thermal pool—is tempting on a raw day; but it's illegal, and extremely dangerous. The water temperature can rise too sharply, and too fast, for escape.

Since nobody was camped downstream, I risked a wash in Shoshone Creek, which winds through the basin. In theory you can select a spot where a hot thermal stream empties into the frigid creek in just the right combination for comfort. In practice, even if you escape scalding, you're reminded of a planet close to the sun: One side freezes while the other boils. You whirl, dance, and shout. You move like a washing-machine agitator: up, down, round and round. At best it's painful, but on a long wilderness trip to feel clean is to feel free.

The next morning, Craig and I followed Shoshone Creek into low, forested mountains. We had a route in mind. But, as often happens on casual walks, especially in the wilderness, we were lured into stopping short of our destination.

What stopped us first was nothing more than a meadow. Shoshone Creek, small here, was joined by a still smaller, nameless tributary. We paused for a snack of nuts and raisins and didn't leave until darkness, five hours later.

Craig noticed it first: a perfect waterfall, the size of his palm, with a pebble "keeper" at its base. Then I saw a fish—not a twenty-inch trout, but a two-inch minnow, resting in tiny plants above a two-inch gravel bar. The entire meadow was a miniature version of the water world we had lived in, and been dwarfed by, for a year. The change of scale was exhilarating. High in the meadow near the edge of the lodgepole forest, the streams progressed gracefully, looping in lazy meanders reminiscent of the enormous oxbows on the Green River. Here we traversed the loops in single strides.

We fashioned canoes from grass blades, and made aspen-leaf rafts. Away they floated, bouncing and spinning past embryo islands, into and out of cameo canyons, ever downward. None ever made it to the confluence. The ones that weren't "kept" at Craig Falls were smashed in a "pebble garden" and sank there.

The most enchanting discovery was a clear pool fringed by overhanging meadow grass. At the bottom, in the brown sand, six miniature springs bubbled intermittently. Each eruption kicked up a small storm of multicolored gravel, pink and charcoal-hued and yellow and gray. The gravel settled slowly back to the bottom, as synthetic snow settles over a Christmas scene in a glass paperweight. We gazed at this for a good hour before we departed.

The next morning we canoed out. Lovely high-flying lenticular clouds were streaking the dark sky silver. We boomed across Shoshone Lake with a good following wind. Swans, fifty or more to the flock, fluttered and flew up as we approached. Slowly they circled the entire lake. Before they landed again we were out of sight, drawn down the channel and out across Lewis Lake.

For a month it had seemed we were alone in the Rocky Mountains. The year, bent at the end of autumn, was giving way to winter. The next visitors would arrive as silently as we departed—but on cross-country skis.

Salvaging the author's breakfast, an alert California gull grips a beakful of pancake. "After downing three," says Ron, "that bird managed to lift off." Park regulations forbid voluntary feeding of animals.

Bull moose vie for dominance in a meadow near the Snake River as the rutting season begins. "The bull on the right was the smaller," says Sam, "but the aggressor. He repeatedly approached and confronted the other. They would spar, and then ramble off

separately, and then come together and clash again. This went on for an hour. I could hear the antlers meet—a strong click and scrape sound." Shed after the rut and regrown yearly, antlers may develop a spread as wide as four feet and weigh as much as 50 pounds to a pair.

*W*et-suited against life-threatening cold, sternman A. J. DeRosa and his friend Richard Murphy hurtle Big Kahuna, a major rapid on the Snake. Water temperature hovers near 40° F. "In this weather you shouldn't run rapids in open canoes without wet suits," says Sam. "They keep you from freezing to death if you spill." The rating for Big Kahuna varies between class II ("easy") and V; it rises to V—"significant hazard to life"—in August, when the water levels create maximum turbulence. The Snake River Canyon in Bridger-Teton National Forest challenges boaters with half a dozen tough rapids in a stretch of 15 miles. In the May-to-October season of 1976, about 56,000 people accepted the risk, but 88 percent signed up with commercial outfitters for raft trips; fewer than 6,000 dared the rapids in smaller craft of their own.

*A*fter a strenuous hour on the cold rapids of the Snake, Craig and A.J. (behind the bow) push a 60-pound canoe up the rocky bank to Richard. Its bow still carries the driftwood patch applied after Ron's Big Swim. A climb of about 20 feet awaits the party — and then a quarter-mile hike, with canoes and gear, through brush and woodland to a gravel access road. "In this country," comments Sam, "an enthusiast can make his own trail." Canyon terrain, however, limits the choice of put-in and take-out points. Some 75 miles upriver by boatmen's reckoning lies Jackson Lake, where a canvasback duck paddles briskly among golden reflections.

With a surgeon's intensity — and a makeshift rig — A. J. reties his spruce streamer, a fly popular for lake fishing. He clamped the hook in a pair of Vise-Grip pliers, then propped their handle in the spout of a coffeepot filled with water for stability. Here he secures a feather to the hook with knots of dental floss from Sam's toilet kit. Casting in the shallows of a lake in Yellowstone, he proves his mettle with a strike. Craig, as chef for the evening, cooked A. J.'s brown trout to flaky perfection on a griddle. Browns spawn in autumn, at season's end.

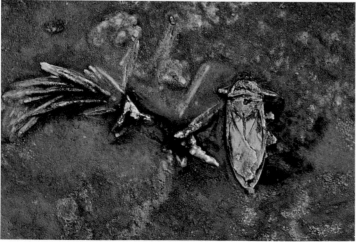

"*O*ur first sighting . . . and a dazzling one," says Sam, recalling this view of Shoshone Geyser Basin at dusk. Wisps and clouds of steam rise from the slopes where trickles of hot runoff find their way to a hot stream; beyond heated ground lie traces of unmelted snow. Pungent sulphurous gases permeate the air

—"it smelled good to me," Sam
confesses. Thermal areas in the
backcountry of Yellowstone lack
the guardrails and boardwalks of
the main tourist centers. Minerals
from thermal waters rime a giant
waterbug and a sprig of lodgepole
pine (left), and thicken the
milky deposits at a geyser pool.

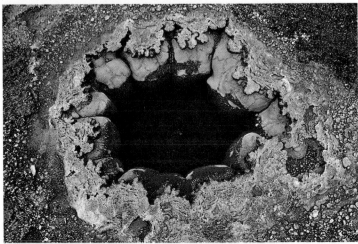

Dreamy haze, well known to morning canoeists, lifts slowly from Shoshone Lake. These fishermen from Colorado have returned for 11 consecutive years. "It's a ritual for them," explains Sam. "They always come the first week of November. They like the solitude

—and we respected their privacy." More than two million people visit Yellowstone each year; comparatively few venture far into the backcountry or risk an early winter storm. "To me this was the most pleasing canoe trip," Sam reminisces. "One I would do again."

6

Endless Days on an Arctic River

SEVENTY MILES ABOVE THE ARCTIC CIRCLE, with the jagged peaks of Alaska's Brooks Range rising around us, our little plane dipped and bobbed in the turbulent mountain winds. A canoe lashed to one of the pontoons was exerting drag. Our pilot showed us the constant compensation it required; he removed his right foot from the rudder pedal, and we lurched sideways as if caught in some invisible river's "instant and terrible force." He restored the trim promptly to keep us from spiraling into the bleak solitude below.

We flew in a thin layer of clear sky—just over the mountains, just under the pale gray clouds, toward the headwaters of the 435-mile-long Noatak River. It rises in the Brooks Range and runs westward toward Siberia, emptying into Kotzebue Sound.

Beneath us, trails made by Dall sheep wound along the desolate ridges, and tiny white streams tumbled and splashed down the sides of the mountains. The pilot searched for a clear route, probing into canyons that were beginning to fill with clouds.

"There's where the Noatak starts," he shouted above the engine's roar, pointing out a white glacier on the slope of Mount Igikpak, at 8,510 feet the highest peak in this part of the range. At its base the Noatak set off on its trip to the sea. Here in its headwaters, the river rambles along in a U-shaped valley two miles wide, its floor scarred by old meanders and by oxbow lakes. The river looked shallow and placid, its braids and branches threading among gravel islands. It looked a little as if it had been designed by a man who had heard descriptions of rivers but had never seen one.

We headed downstream to the first lake large enough to land on, a nameless one about a mile by a half-mile. With a sigh the

Glow of an ebbing day envelops 12-year-old Carl Wilson in the Eskimo fishing village of Noatak, on the Noatak River. Too young to work with his father in the family boat, Carl fishes the salmon-rich river for fun— and dreams of piloting a Sabrejet some day.

plane settled onto it. I relaxed my grip on the airsickness bag.

Doug Gosling and Nancy Weintrub, a student of entomology who was joining us, waved from the shore. They had flown in the previous afternoon and been stranded when deteriorating weather delayed the rest of us. Still to come were Mike O'Connor, a seventh-grade teacher from Omaha, and our guide. As we taxied up, Doug and Nancy dropped onto all fours in a pantomime of grazing, munching at the short grass—they had brought one of the canoes, two of the tents, and a lot of camping gear, but no food.

I had never been this far north—indeed, had never expected to reach the Arctic Circle, let alone cross it—and impressions came almost faster than I could deal with them.

"No trees!" was my first thought. The valley sloped upward to the mountains with only occasional clumps of dwarf willow and brush. Grasses and mosses covered the thin active layer of soil that thaws in summer; beneath lay permafrost, perennially frozen ground. The turf felt spongy to walk on, a little like a freshly plowed field. The permafrost stops water from seeping downward, which contributes to the sponginess and also helps to account for the numerous lakes, ponds, and puddles on the tundra.

The most astonishing feature I discovered after supper, later that night when darkness failed to fall. At midnight the light reminded me of a cloudy afternoon in Washington. The sun would set, but barely, leaving the landscape cold and shadowless. The curious, round-the-clock daylight would stay with us for much of our month-long trip, and it never failed to surprise me when I woke at one in the morning and found light enough to read by. A pallid silver moon would pass overhead, but the stars remained hidden. Every day the sun sank lower beneath the horizon, so by the end of the trip we were getting good solid darkness.

Sam had put us onto the Noatak as a likely canoeing river, attracted by the chance to journey the entire length of such a river—from source to mouth—without encountering the works of man. The Noatak drainage is one of the biggest in North America still virtually untouched by human influences, he said.

After leaving the peaks, the Noatak winds across a vast plain, with only a few rapids where the river crosses ancient moraines. Ten lesser rivers flow into it, as well as 40 named creeks—all of them virtually untouched by man. The Noatak basin actually straddles the boundary between the tundra of the Arctic and the taiga—or coniferous forest—of the Subarctic, so their wildlife and vegetation overlap, contributing to the ecological richness.

In 1973 a team of scientists from the Center for Northern Studies in Wolcott, Vermont, spent the summer studying the Noatak basin. As their director, Steven B. Young, wrote later, they found most impressive "the vastness and timeless quality of the region." They were amazed "at the variety of both large habitat and microenvironment." They stressed the size of the basin, "a true wilderness rather than an enclave of wild country surrounded by civilization on all sides," and its uniqueness—"there is certainly no situation left in the lower 48 that is remotely comparable. The Noatak valley and the surrounding countryside afford one of the last opportunities in the United States, or for that matter the entire world, to set aside for the future a wilderness of such size, variability, and complexity that it functions as a complete ecosystem."

Dr. Young stressed a point that grows more timely with the recent development of oil fields in northern Alaska: "One of the first things you have to keep in mind is that when you take a piece of wilderness and put a road through it, you don't end up with two smaller pieces of wilderness, necessarily. You often end up with no wilderness at all."

Currently before Congress is a proposal recommending the addition of 83.5 million acres of Alaska to the national systems of parks, forests, wildlife refuges, and wild and scenic rivers. The bill would create a 7.6 million-acre Noatak National Arctic Range.

I caught a hint of its vastness when our pilot scanned the lowering clouds and said, "I probably won't be back tonight. I'll try to get back in the morning with the others." When his plane had disappeared, the silence was as complete as I've ever experienced. There was literally no sound whatever.

"I guess on this trip we won't hear any more airplanes or Interstate Highways or chain saws," said Sam, and indeed we didn't.

That night we had a first brush with a renowned Alaskan— the tundra mosquito. We had been warned—indeed, nearly intimidated—by tales of this awesome insect. There were stories of game driven mad by mosquitoes, and tourists driven home. In summer, the pests can drain as much as a quart of blood a week from a caribou. Nancy offered another bit of hearsay: "Somebody once said that if there were any more mosquitoes in Alaska, they'd have to be smaller." We found the creatures plentiful but slow; no need to swat, just smear them across your forehead.

In the morning, after a night of blustery showers, the rest of our party flew in and we walked a mile or so to a pingo—a symmetrical hill like a giant haystack that is a characteristic tundra feature. A pingo forms when a tundra lake fills with silt. Permafrost

Crossing treeless tundra and forested taiga north of the Arctic Circle, the Noatak meanders 435 miles through the Brooks Range before emptying into Kotzebue Sound. Its name, corrupted from the Eskimo, roughly corresponds to "Deeper Within."

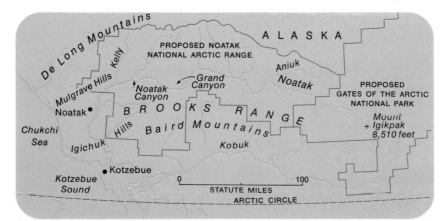

encroaches from the sides, and the center freezes. Unable to expand sideways, the lake water bulges upward as it freezes. Eventually, an ice-cored mound is formed.

Caribou antlers, discarded like the baggage of a retreating army, littered the tundra, with tiny delicate wild flowers blooming among them and toadstools here and there.

Ground squirrels — sand-colored, with five-inch tails — skittered along the skyline of the pingo as we approached, scurrying like townspeople who sight an attacking army. A raw gouge on the pingo's flank showed where a bear had dug into their burrows, and at the top we saw only the gaping mouths of the little tunnels. Later I noticed that even in the endless days of summer, ground squirrels seem to observe a punctual bedtime; they retired around 9 p.m. and came out about 4 a.m. In autumn they line their nests with fur lost by migrating caribou, and they hibernate during the winter.

We went on to make an arduous climb of about 3,000 feet to the valley's rim, resting beside a trickling stream where a young caribou waded and clattered on the stones. Through our binoculars we spotted flocks of Dall sheep browsing on distant slopes. We counted 34 of them in all, a few near enough for stalking along the barren heights. Herds of caribou moseyed along the ridges and crests.

Doug, a student of botany, stopped often to examine the tiny delicate vegetation. "Everything's dwarf," he said. "There're dwarf willows and dwarf birch. And every step we climb takes us a little farther north, botanically. Some plants have stayed with us clear to the top, though. Up here they're just a little dwarfier."

Below us, the valley spread out like a map. Lakes and ponds followed the meandering river. We could just see our tents, little spots of orange and green like tiny blossoms on the edge of our lake. Stately cloud shadows as big as the mountains flowed down the valley.

Bumblebees and little gray grasshoppers buzzed and hopped back in the quiet valley among the sedge tussocks. "This particular sedge doesn't spread," Doug explained. "It keeps growing right on top of itself, so you get these tussocks, clumps several inches high. Many tundra plants don't even have common names," he went on. "And they're incredibly adapted to their environment. Frozen seeds of Arctic lupine will still grow; some that produced healthy plants were found in frozen silt 10,000 years old."

Yet the tundra is very fragile, slow to recover from abuse. One archeological site 2,000 years old is still visible from the air; the willow brush nearby has not yet reestablished itself.

We worked carefully next morning, the last day of July, as we carted our canoes and cargo a couple of hundred yards through the tangled head-high willows to the Noatak. This far up, the river was hardly wider than a country lane.

It was five o'clock in the afternoon when we finally got the canoes loaded and launched — but with no threat of darkness we felt no pressure to hurry. We floated along, happy to be in the canoes again, passing clumps of willow on the banks and gravel bars on every turn and meander. Crying terns swept overhead. Little streams and creeks came rushing to join us, giggling over rocky beds.

Midas Creek entered on our right, a reminder that prospectors were here at the turn of the century. They coined hopeful names— Midas Creek, Lucky Six Creek—but found little gold.

Three weeks of canoeing lay between us and our first destination, the Eskimo village of Noatak, the only settlement on the river, about 70 miles from the mouth. The awesome landscape of the tundra unrolled before us, and the days passed with solemn beauty, with hours of joyous canoeing and a few moments of fear.

I remember pulling onto a gravel bar with Sam to camp, about 10 p.m. As we waited for the others, I glanced at the brush lining the beach and there stood a fox, blending with the bushes in the shadowless dusk. His fur was abundant, reddish in the dimness, and he held a large bird in his mouth. He paused with his back to us, regarding us over one shoulder, for a long moment. Then with a move so stealthy and quick it was hard to see, he was gone.

The weather was a sustained surprise. Often we traveled in shorts and T-shirts. It seemed odd to be here, high above the Arctic Circle, worrying about sweat-soaked clothes and sunburned noses. The water in the river, on the other hand, was frigid, maybe 45° F. Not so long ago it had been ice, after all. Even a minute of wading to launch the canoes left our feet aching from the cold.

"Without a wet suit you wouldn't last ten minutes in this water," Mike warned us. So we vowed to be careful.

Trying to keep track of our progress, I found that many of the hills and valleys were nameless, merely contour lines on the map. We named a treeless symmetrical dome "Mount Baldy," after Sam, but couldn't agree on names to honor the rest of us.

Wildlife surrounded us. Four grizzlies ambled and waddled along a mountainside, munching blueberries. Beyond them grazed 30 Dall sheep. We saw caribou every day—in herds or solitary— passing on ridges near the river or trotting along gravel bars. I marveled at the antlers on some of them, huge racks seemingly beyond anything useful or necessary, antlers so towering and heavy I expected the creatures to collapse and fall forward onto their faces.

The mud along the shore was scribbled everywhere with tracks of caribou, birds, and bears. One set of footprints—a fox's, I think—was so neatly and gently imprinted we could see the impression of the individual hairs between the pads of the feet.

With little distinction between night and day, we began traveling later and later, once eating supper at midnight with plenty of light to see by. Sam has had years of experience at assessing light, but one morning he got up at 4:30 a.m., thinking it was much later. He built a fire, made coffee, and brought it to the tents for us. Puzzled but willing, wondering about a possible emergency, we all got up, a good four hours earlier than usual.

Mosquitoes became more troublesome as we descended from the mountains. Usually a cloud hovered (Continued on page 174)

Watery oxbows and braids sprawl restlessly across the two-mile-wide Noatak Valley near the river's source in the Brooks Range. Fed by melting snows and glaciers, its main stream and tributaries drain more than 12,000 square miles of untamed land, making

this one of the largest mountain-ringed wilderness basins in North America. Unlike other "wilderness areas," it remains remote from civilization, not surrounded by it. Scientists especially value its variety of climate and terrain and habitat for large and small animals.

"*Every day, we saw caribou. Each campsite had antlers and other sign,*" recalls the author. *A lone female lopes along river's edge; expedition members Mike O'Connor (left) and Doug Gosling examine a caribou antler they found buried in a gravel bar; mud preserves a hoofprint fringed by cracks. The animal's apparent abundance, however, belies an alarming*

DOUG GOSLING (BELOW)

decline. *During the past six years, one estimated population has dropped from 250,000 to a mere fraction, something between 60,000 and 50,000 — and no one knows precisely why. The caribou crisis seriously threatens the people of Alaska's inland villages, where hunters still depend heavily on the animal for food in winter.*

Like ocean combers that endlessly wax and wane offshore, rolling cloud banks rim the Noatak Valley high above canoeists Doug Gosling and Nancy Weintrub. Here, fifty miles downstream, the widening river cuts through somewhat gentler terrain; landscapes continue

to flatten with each passing mile. Setting out in late July, the party successfully avoided bad weather during their month-long trip. "It was the Arctic," comments Ron. "But it felt like spring in Virginia. We had a lot of T-shirt days—and a lot of sunburn."

around everyone's head. The repellent kept them off pretty well, and their buzzing was often the only sound in the stillness.

We caught a few fish — grayling, mostly, which reminded me of trout — to supplement the food we had packed in. A ground squirrel hunkered down and watched me fish one day; he sat in the crumbling mud of the bank, gathering dead grass for his nest. Fat and sleek, he snatched it with quick little jerks — as if impatient to see me land a fish — but we were both disappointed.

Gradually our valley disappeared, opening up to broad, rolling tundra. Great swinging meanders carried us across the Aniuk Lowland, a shallow bowl that slopes gently upward from the river. A lowland it may be, but we were still about a thousand feet above sea level. We saw the river at work: Crumbling banks several feet high dropped chunks of sod into the water. Once we heard the musical *plink plank plunk* of sand dribbling from the bank into the river.

In the Aniuk Lowland we had the finest, most exhilarating canoeing of our entire year. When a river rounds a bend, the water is usually deepest near the outside bank. Here, with the water level low, the sloping bottom was exposed, and the river often broke up into several braids with gravel bars between them. The current cut downgrade and "sideways" across and among these bars in narrow channels. Running very fast, it carried us whooping and yelling through the braids.

Usually the three canoes took different routes, to race around the bend. You could glance sideways and see two disembodied heads a quarter of a mile away, hurtling along just above a gravel bar. The rocky bottom, a few inches away, flickered beneath us at a dizzying speed. With the water so shallow there was no danger — "low-stress canoeing" we called it — and I've never had more fun in a canoe than I did in that 30-mile stretch in the Aniuk Lowland.

Even mischance could be fun. Sam and I got stuck on some rocks in a riffle, with that ice-cold water frothing past us. "I'll get out," said Sam, in the stern, and he did. He freed the stern and got back in. The bow held fast, and the current swung the canoe around, facing us upstream. "I'll get out," I said, and gritted my teeth. I rocked us free, got back in — and away we went, backward through the rest of the riffle.

There came a day when the Noatak, until then a frolicsome, frisky river, turned treacherous. We had breakfasted early — and heartily — on oatmeal Mike had prepared. Misreading the directions, he had fixed enough to feed a Boy Scout troop. We had two big helpings apiece and still there was a pan full, a big pan.

"Save it," said Nancy, "and I'll make oatcakes tonight." So I paddled that day with a pan of cold oatmeal wedged beneath the seat. We ran rapids for hours, short stretches of boulder gardens that were fine entertainment. Doug and I, in the lead canoe, were in the midst of one when we romped around a bend and the old, unmistakable roar hit us. Suddenly we were in waves much too large for an undecked, heavily loaded canoe.

Water cascaded over the bow into Doug's lap and we lurched sideways. *"Paddle!"* I shouted, and we drove furiously to the right, crossing the flank of the V and just missing the worst of the waves. With six inches of water in the canoe—and just seconds from foundering—we edged our bow into an eddy near the shore. The current swung us around and parked us neatly in shallow water.

"They're out!" shouted Doug. I looked around to see Sam clinging to the upturned canoe, Nancy bobbing in its wake. No life jackets, freezing water, our canoe—the nearest rescue craft—barely afloat. They swept past us as we stood dumbfounded. Nancy struck out for the opposite shore, swimming hard, and was soon wading onto a gravel bar. Sam stayed with the canoe for another fifty yards before the current washed him onto the beach.

Doug had sprinted off to stay abreast of him, shouting encouragement. I had grabbed the oatmeal pan, emptied it into the river, and started bailing frantically. Doug dashed back, and we got our canoe across the river at our best speed to find Sam and Nancy without cuts or fractures but chilled through, shivering uncontrollably. Mike and the guide came up—they had seen us in trouble and had beached their canoe upstream of the rapid. Doug snatched dry clothes from his pack for Nancy and Sam, and we assessed the damage to supplies. A paddle missing; a pair of Nancy's boots; some gloves. Everything in that canoe soaked or lost. The packs, lashed in, had stayed aboard; but many of Sam's cameras and lenses were either gone or ruined.

Hastily we got ourselves downstream to a spot where a tangle of brush had captured a huge jumble of dry driftwood. As Mike got a fire blazing and Doug started some soup, I set up the tents. Though Sam had more cameras safe in waterproof cases, the loss of equipment and exposed film left him dejected, almost demoralized.

"I had the loaded cameras right at my feet," he told me. "I didn't realize we were in trouble till I saw waves washing over them. I wasted a few precious seconds just staring at them, trying to decide whether to save them or the canoe. By then it was too late."

And things didn't get any better. As soon as we got all the wet sleeping bags and clothes spread out on the bushes to dry, it began to rain. That was the emotional low point of the trip. Everyone was shaken by mishap, aware of what might have happened, distrustful now of our playful river: If there's one big rapid, are there more? We sat around the fire that night in a waning drizzle with wet sleeping bags across our knees, trying to fluff up clumps of soggy down.

It rained all night, and next morning we were even lower. Rain had turned the campsite to grit and mud. Puddles of water glistened on my plate as I stood, hooded and shivering, waiting for the oatmeal to bubble. My boots were soaked and full of sand. There was nothing to sit on. Wet packs, stowed under wet tarps, bulged with wet socks and wet sweaters.

We pressed on for a few hours that day, camped in the rain again, and shivered that night in sleeping bags still wet and lumpy.

But it only takes a little sunshine to turn things around. The morning dawned hot and clear, and we spread everything in the sun and dispersed along a mile-long beach, bathing, shampooing, working on our tans. From Sam's bathing spot down the river came the sound of his lusty tenor: "Lord, I Feel like Going Home."

Mike, the first one up that morning, had made us pancakes. He was an unassuming young man who, for the past two years, had saved enough from his teacher's salary for a backpacking or canoeing trip in Alaska. We found out later—on the last day of the trip—that he had played football for the University of Nebraska, an accomplishment I would have managed to mention on the first day.

As we sat eating his pancakes he told us about seeing a fox. "I was gathering more firewood when I saw him walking slowly toward me. I knelt down, and he passed by close enough to be petted. He sat for a while and gazed at the fire, probably thinking about fish. The two I caught last night are missing from the bush where we hung them. I guess the fox was coming back for seconds."

We put into the water that night after supper, to see how late we could travel now that the nights were somewhat darker. With a good current and tailwind we made about 20 miles. At first we headed into the glare of the setting sun; it finally dipped behind a mountain about ten o'clock, and the sky colors softened and darkened, from blue to gray, as a nearly full moon rose behind us. Still the stars stayed hidden. The shore gradually grew fainter—a mere dark line in the distance—until we seemed suspended on a timeless, soundless, empty stream, with moonbeams glinting faintly like veiled diamonds on the water at our paddles. About 12:30, when it began to get chilly, we stopped and had some soup and went to bed.

That was a particularly clear evening. On other days it was as though a gifted child had found a cloudmaking machine and wanted to try one of each. We saw scudding and tumbling clouds, wispy clouds and dense clouds, white, gray, purplish clouds, high-rise clouds and pancake-thin clouds. Light from above played across them, seeking crevices and breaks. A distant mountain would suddenly brighten and glow. Cloud shadows would slide over peaks and down the sides of hills, curling around the mountaintops like fog. Against a gray heaven, a dazzling white seagull would wing past, sounding its outraged cry. Two or three rain squalls would glower in the distance. One day a perfect rainbow developed a twin and suddenly there were two perfect rainbows, arching one above the other. One afternoon we were under an enormous blue gap in the sky—with clouds all around but none above—and the blue sent us a gentle, uncanny mist.

We paddled through the Grand Canyon of the Noatak, 65 miles long. At times its undulating walls are barely visible, well back from the river. Arctic terns hovered overhead, crying in alarm or anger, swooping and darting at upraised paddles. The weather stayed clear, and enormous skies with clouds the size of Rhode Island covered us with a canopy of silence, splashed us now and then with shafts of hot sunshine. Flocks of geese, heading south, swept above us, honking. The light seemed to mellow as it sank into the green, humid tundra.

I've never been in a place where the sense of vastness and solitude was so overwhelming, so humbling. Often the only sound was the beating of our own hearts. After weeks of exposure to the enormous and empty country our senses seemed almost to rebel; we needed the periods of darkness and of snugness—the security of a manageable habitat—that our tents offered. Yet I wished that I could know this land in the dead of winter, with the snow deep and the temperature as much as 140 degrees lower.

At one chilly campsite, everyone had a column of mosquitoes twenty feet high hovering overhead. In the perfect stillness, heat from our bodies rose straight upward and the mosquitoes seemed to park there as if trying to escape the chill.

"They're zeroing in on us," Nancy explained. "They use heat and smell to help locate their prey. They seem to use the carbon dioxide we give off, too, but nobody's sure how."

I remembered the story of a naturalist working with a native helper in Nicaragua. "Sir," said the helper, "can you tell me what is the use of mosquitoes?" "To enjoy themselves and be happy." "Ah, sir, if I was only a mosquito!"

Gnats, too, appeared. One day they were there in their millions, sounding like a sprinkle of rain as they battered themselves against the tent, living their brief season under the waning sun.

By now signs of autumn were appearing—lighter green patches on the tundra, as plants began to fade and go dormant; yellow and rust leaves on the dwarf willows. We reached the tree line and passed a solitary stand of spruce, the first honest-to-goodness trees we had seen in two weeks. The sound of the wind in their branches was like a greeting from an old friend.

In Noatak Canyon, a precipitous gorge 200 to 300 feet deep, we stopped to fish where a little stream emptied into the river. "If this canyon were somewhere in the Lower 48," said Sam, "we'd have seen postcards of this place. *(Continued on page 184)*

From porcupines that lumbered along the banks "like miniature grizzlies" to acrobatic Arctic terns that were "confident to the point of cockiness," creatures of the Noatak impressed Sam Abell with a complete lack of fear. Such boldness may stem in part from the fact that man remains an infrequent visitor here. Perhaps only a few score people a year travel the river's length. The Noatak's vastness and its wealth of wildlife — grizzly bears, wolves, foxes, Dall sheep, ptarmigan, geese, cranes, and many other animals — have inspired the scientists who study the region. Many believe that its unique importance demands immediate governmental protection. Currently before Congress: a provision to set aside a 7.6-million-acre Noatak National Arctic Range.

Beginner's luck: A nine-pound chum, or dog salmon, and Ron's almost incandescent grin tell the outcome of the day's very first cast. He hooked this prize at a fishing spot popular during summer salmon runs—the confluence of the Noatak and the Kelly River, a tributary. After a ten-minute battle, he worked his catch into the shallows where Mike helped land it. Soon after, salmon steaks sputtered over the fire. The river's bounty of salmon, grayling, and char dictated the campers' usual evening fare—fish steamed on evergreen twigs in a covered pot, and rice cooked in a wok. In good years salmon abound in such numbers here that the Eskimos—who prefer the taste of female salmon—often feed the males to their dogs.

A poncho her only shelter, Nancy Weintrub quietly accepts the aggravations of cooking in a wilderness kitchen: Rain and insects annoy the chef, campfires burn too hot or die too soon, food sticks to the pots (which always seem to outnumber the cooking spaces), and someone forgot to pack the marjoram! Somehow she succeeds in setting forth a feast, often using local foods. Blueberries gleaned from the tundra simmer in a wok (above) before becoming part of a tempting double-crust pie, baked in a makeshift Dutch oven.

It's nice not to have 'previews of scenic highlights.' Here we can discover them for ourselves."

Mike caught five grayling with five casts, but by the time I got my rod assembled the feeding frenzy was over. Not even a nibble.

At the mouth of the Kelly River my day as a fisherman finally came. I cast my lure into the roiling brown river and was immediately yanked forward onto my toes by a powerful lunge. "Zzzzzzzz" went the line cascading from my reel, and I knew I had hooked something accustomed to having its own way. The fish fought and leaped and ran for ten minutes, as I cranked furiously to play him and yelled for help and moral support. I would work him within a few feet of shore, only to have him swerve and dash once more into midstream. Finally, exhausted, he came to rest, gasping, in the shallows, and Mike helped me land him. Vindicated as an angler at last, I pulled in my nine-pound salmon. We dined memorably that night on fresh salmon steaks, fried in butter and lemon juice.

We had a less dramatic encounter when we encircled a porcupine that came to the river to drink. He seemed more annoyed than afraid; he turned one way, then another, but slowly. Obviously he couldn't decide whether we had him surrounded or he had us buffaloed. As we stood and talked gibberish to him, he yawned, perhaps from anxiety. We relented, and he ambled toward some trees without a backward glance.

We reached the Mission Lowland, a broad expanse of tundra sprinkled with lakes and ponds. We were bounded on the south by the Igichuk Hills, on the east by the Baird Mountains, on the west by the Mulgrave Hills, on the north by the De Long Mountains. But the nearest peaks were twenty miles away, pale blue humps on the horizon. In its northern and central reaches here the Noatak is a heavily braided river about two miles wide. Pingos rise beside it, ranging from 25 to 300 feet high.

By now we had to be near the village of Noatak; and next evening, as we set up camp, a motorboat pulled ashore. An agile, middle-aged Eskimo stepped out and shook hands all around. "Welcome to the Noatak River," he said.

His name was Edwin Booth, and with him were his wife, their little son, and a fluffy yellow puppy. We explained our trip, and asked the mileage to the village. "There, around the bend," he said, pointing. "It's right around that bend." As the puppy and little boy chased each other about, Edwin explained their presence on the river. "We just go for a ride this nice day. The boy, he likes it." Though he spoke English clearly and fluently, there were hints of another syntax and different rhythms. We told Edwin we looked forward to seeing him in the village, and helped to launch his boat.

A welcoming committee met us on the beach next day, headed by Mrs. Rachel Sherman and a clutch of curious children. She was expecting another party, we learned, but she treated us as guests. The village has a store, air service to Kotzebue, an elementary school, and a church. It was to the church that she led us, for a

Wednesday evening service was about to begin. A frame building, the church was decorated with a faded picture of Jesus on one wall and artificial flowers in pots wrapped with aluminum foil. Parishioners stood, one at a time, spoke of their faith, then selected a hymn they wished to sing. All of the hymns were in English, but some of the older people spoke in Eskimo.

Rachel stood and addressed us: "We'd like to welcome you to Noatak. Whenever we have visitors, we like to welcome them with this song." The entire congregation trooped to the front of the church, the organ burst forth with a chord, and they sang—beautifully—"When We All Get to Heaven."

Another surprise: The Eskimos in Noatak are Quakers.

Long ago the different denominations divided Alaska into mission fields. In 1908 the village of Noatak grew up around a federal school operated by Elmer and Emily Harnden, Quaker missionaries representing the California Yearly Meeting of Friends (headquartered at Whittier). The present mayor's grandfather picked the site. Today the community varies between 200 and 290 people; in summer many of the men fish or hunt seal in Kotzebue Sound.

Carl Wilson, a bright 12-year-old, took me in hand to show me around. An avid reader, he confided his ambitions to me. "I want to be a jet pilot. I read this book about a Sabrejet pilot. That's the best book I ever read. Sometimes I feel bad that I've already read it; now I can't ever enjoy it like I did before."

Change was coming to Noatak. Most of the people lived in log cabins that looked drafty and infirm, but proved to be cozy and snug. But rows of new prefabricated frame houses were going up, financed in part by the Bureau of Indian Affairs. The muddy streets were torn and rutted.

"What's going on here?" I asked Carl.

"Water and sewage lines," he said. "Pretty soon we'll have telephones in all the houses, too."

Snowmobiles were parked alongside disintegrating dogsleds. Once upon a time, the mayor told me later, you could tell you were approaching an Eskimo village by the clamor of the dogs barking, a din that seldom ceased. Today a sound that never stops is the hum of the generator that supplies the village with electricity. Outside one of the new buildings, the Community Hall, a dish antenna stares unblinking at a satellite 22,000 miles away; Noatak is connected to the outside world by a satellite telephone. I made a few calls on it; and the split-second delay between question and response seemed, paradoxically, to emphasize the remoteness of modern Noatak. In season the women go out to gather blueberries. They use hand-carved wooden scoops, possibly designed thousands of years ago, to shake the berries into their buckets, then they take the berries home and store them in new Amana freezers on their porches. (You *can* sell refrigerators to the Eskimos.)

We ate dinner one night with Rachel and her family, dining on caribou steak, mashed potatoes, salad, and a blueberry pie that

Nancy and Doug had baked on the fire at our campsite on the beach. Rachel spoke of the dwindling caribou herd.

"In 1970 there were about 250,000 caribou in our herd. Now, maybe 50,000. Nobody knows for sure where they've gone. Maybe wolves. Maybe Eskimos kill too many with their snowmobiles. Used to be we could kill as many as we needed. A family eats maybe one caribou a week all winter. This year the Fish and Game office issued permits—one permit, one caribou. Noatak got 114 permits to last us all winter. The people gonna starve at that rate.

"But this is good country," she said. "We get just about everything we need in any season. In winter we kill the caribou, catch the trout and graylings and whitefish through the ice on the river. My husband's dad spends the winter at the Kelly River trapping—fox, wolves, wolverine, otter.

"In spring we catch the rabbits and ptarmigans, and when it starts to thaw the geese come. We find seagull nests—little mounds on the islands or the riverbanks—and collect eggs. In summer the men go to the sound and hunt the beluga and seals, and in the fall we seine the river for trout and hunt the caribou. We get what you call Eskimo potatoes—roots that the people find in mouses' caches. Mouses store them for the winter. When the people take them they put in a few crackers or something to replace what they take."

We camped for a few days at Noatak, a constant source of interest for the children, happy youngsters in "Keep On Truckin'" T-shirts and jeans with "Love Me" patches sewn on. They would stand in a circle around our fire; occasionally they burst into giggles when we couldn't see that we'd done anything funny. A friendly dog adopted us. "His master in Kotzebue this summer," Carl told us. "Nobody feeds him." We bought him canned tamales, the nearest thing to dogfood the little store offered. He slept inside our tent.

The children had a violent side, just beneath the surface. Idly fishing with a simple line and hook near our tent, one of the little girls landed a salmon. A dozen youngsters erupted in a frenzy of kicking and stomping, trying to kill the fish before it could flop back into the river. Blood trickled from its mouth as it thrashed in the dirt. In a few moments they had it cut up and hanging over the fire; when it was slightly cooked, they fed it to our adopted dog.

"How do you say good-bye in Eskimo?" I asked Carl when it came time to go. But he didn't know. The language, though taught in the school, is spoken mostly by the elders. We left with only our dog and three teenage girls to see us off. The dog ran along the beach, wagging his tail, then sat and watched us out of sight.

Below Noatak the river widens and slows dramatically. The current has long since dropped its load of rocks, so the beaches are sand or mud. We took several days to make the seventy miles to Kotzebue Sound, battling mosquitoes, scaring up sandhill cranes.

We had time to meditate on the river, time for minor diversions and minor annoyances. We wondered at the age of the water, and learned later that it might have melted from snow a century old.

One day Sam climbed a hill to make photographs and reported to us, "I was awash—*a-knee*—in blueberries!" We picked a bagful and had a light supper of blueberry muffins and coffee.

Mosquitoes came to be more troublesome, clustering around us as if for warmth. I fished 13 out of a cup of coffee one night, before I could get it consumed.

Daily now, in the afternoon, we faced a wind blowing upstream. Once when it kicked up a chop and became too strong for paddling, we got out and towed our canoes through the shallows.

"Is the Noatak the perfect canoeing river?" Sam asked one day, and we talked about that. It's a long way from almost anywhere, we decided; it's expensive to get to it, the weather is unpredictable, and there's only a short summer season.

On the other hand, it's generally a safe and shallow river, with beautiful clear water; its riffles and rapids are fun; it's so isolated that there're no crowds; there're lots of wildlife and magnificent scenery—and clean and plentiful campsites on the gravel bars.

A few days later the Noatak—now nearly a sea—slowed us and tired us and confused us with islands, and finally relinquished us, the merest motes in the eye of the Great Land, to Kotzebue Sound, an arm of the Chukchi Sea, a branch of the Arctic Ocean. Its waters never lose their chill. Night fell as we paddled for ten miles across the sound. Lightning flickered from rain squalls on the horizon, and rollers hissed and feathered at our paddles, and the lights of Kotzebue seemed never to get any closer.

The scale of the sound seemed to match the scale of the land we had just left, and we felt lost and helpless on the ice-blue water.

Nevertheless, paddling automatically, I would think back on our travels, think of our canoeing companions and wish they were here. We had tested a lot of waters—and been tested by some—and our brave and tattered canoes deserved a rest.

About 10 p.m. we reached Kotzebue, with the pale green northern lights flickering and dancing and undulating directly overhead, and we hugged one another and danced in a circle beneath them.

Looked at bow on, our canoes' sides curved inward, trying to form a circle. That inward curvature is called the tumblehome. Tumblehome, a foolish but fetching word for something so mechanical, I always thought.

And I thought of it again now. Tumblehome. That's about what we did.

Summer's bane, the notorious Alaskan mosquito overpopulates the Noatak in plague proportions. One night, 20-foot-high columns of the noisy pests swarmed above each repellent-smeared camper, apparently drawing warmth from their intended prey.

Arrayed in Sunday best, six-year-old Amelia Sherman of Noatak village welcomes the canoeists for dinner at her home. After a service at the Quaker meetinghouse, neighbor Nellie Woods (above) invited them home for doughnuts and coffee. A settled community since 1908, when the government founded a school for the nomadic Eskimos, Noatak remains the river's only town. Many of its 290 residents still hunt, trap, or fish for a living, but increasingly favor new conveniences: snowmobiles, prefab houses, satellite telephones, and an airstrip with flights to Kotzebue.

Stalled by mounting headwinds and lagging currents, Ron and Doug tow their canoes through broad shallows about thirty miles downstream from Noatak village. "The river had grown so big it was like a lake," recalls Ron. "We could walk faster than we could paddle, and

the water wasn't too cold, so off came our shoes." Their forced march lasted only a few hours, however. Although the Noatak widens and splits into several channels as it crosses this region, it soon rejoins itself. Then it narrows to rush through a stony gorge in the Igichuk Hills.

"*A place of solitude*" — *so Park Service planner John M. Kauffmann describes the Noatak, where abstract erosion patterns punctuate a sand flat, and dandelion-like heads of cotton grass in seed crowd the shoreline. Such delicate tapestries of Nature texture the entire valley with a subtle, timeless beauty. Summertime further enhances the river's gentle magic, for then the skies never completely darken. Hilltops smolder a deep pink as the midnight sun dips briefly below the horizon, then ascends with each new day.*

Final sunset of the journey illumines Doug on Kotzebue Sound, a small but deceptive arm of the Arctic Ocean. Having reached the Noatak's mouth, the voyagers headed across the sound toward the town of Kotzebue—and near tragedy. The course took far longer than they

anticipated; for three tense hours they paddled in darkness, fighting contrary winds and fears of being swamped or swept out to sea. "It was the worst part of the trip," Ron said later. "We were so glad to get ashore that we leaped out of the canoes and danced a jig of joy."

Index

Acknowledgments

The Special Publications Division is grateful to the individuals, agencies, and organizations named or quoted in this book, and to those cited here, for their generous cooperation and help during its preparation: the Smithsonian Institution; the U. S. Department of Agriculture—the National Arboretum, Bridger-Teton National Forest, Superior National Forest; the U. S. Department of the Interior—Bureau of Land Management (Utah office), Bureau of Outdoor Recreation, Grand Portage National Monument, Grand Teton National Park, Yellowstone National Park; State of Alaska—Cooperative Wildlife Research Unit, Department of Fish and Game, Department of Natural Resources; State of Florida—Division of Recreation and Parks of the Department of Natural Resources; State of Georgia—Department of Natural Resources; State of Maine—Bureau of Parks and Recreation; Utah State Geologist Dr. Donald T. McMillan; the American National Red Cross; the Montana State Historical Society; and Pearl Baker, Bill Belknap, Dr. Walter Cottam, Clyde C. Council, Dr. James M. Crawford, Dr. C. D. Ellis, Dr. Edwin S. Hall, Jr., and Dr. Arthur O. Roberts.

Additional References

"There is *nothing*—absolutely nothing—half so much worth doing as simply messing about in boats. Simply messing." So says Water Rat in Kenneth Grahame's *The Wind in the Willows.*

Whether simply messing about, or tripping, or competing, canoeing is indeed worth doing. And there are several organizations in the United States that will help you to do it safely and with competence.

The American Canoe Association (4260 E. Evans Avenue, Denver, Colorado 80222) provides an advisory service for members as well as educational and training services and a list of local organizations offering instruction. Membership in this, the largest and oldest canoe club in the United States, includes a subscription to *Canoe* magazine, published bimonthly.

The United States Canoe Association (606 Ross Street, Middletown, Ohio 45042) sponsors competitions, cruising events, educational, safety and conservation programs, and publishes *Canoe News* bimonthly.

The American Whitewater Affiliation (P.O. Box 321, Concord, New Hampshire 03301) leans toward rapid-running with emphasis on safety; it publishes *American Whitewater Journal* bimonthly.

These organizations will assist you in locating the local canoe clubs that exist by the dozen around the country. There is sure to be one in your state.

Most state governments also publish brochures and pamphlets for canoeists. Try writing your state's Department of Natural Resources, Fish and Game Commission, or Department of Conservation.

Numerous general books about canoeing exist, so check your library's card catalog. Verne Huser, *River Running*; Rick Kemmer, *A Guide to Paddle Adventure*; Robert E. McNair, *Basic River Canoeing*; Bill Riviere, *Pole, Paddle & Portage: A Complete Guide to Canoeing* —all were exceedingly helpful in preparing this book. The American National Red Cross has prepared a basic and authoritative text entitled *Canoeing*.

If you don't canoe but would like to, contact your chapter of the American National Red Cross. Many local chapters conduct 12- to 20-hour courses in canoeing, with just a small charge for their textbook and perhaps a canoe rental fee.

The U. S. Geological Survey offers free indexes showing the topographic maps of each state, excellent for use by canoeists. These may be obtained from the Branch of Distribution. If you want maps for areas east of the Mississippi, write to 1200 S. Eads Street, Arlington, Virginia 22202; for areas west of that river, write to Box 25286 Denver Federal Center, Denver, Colorado 80225. Charts of some waterways can also be purchased from the U. S. Army Corps of Engineers.

The rivers of America belong to you and me, but the bottoms may not. State laws differ on who owns the actual riverbed, so you may be canoeing on private property. Treat it accordingly. In many farming areas, landowners run their fences across streams, to keep livestock within their property lines. These fences can be a hazard or a nuisance to canoeists, but should be left alone. In many cases, portages, access points, campsites, and springs are on private land, and permission to use them should be requested before setting out.

As in all wilderness travel, care should be taken to minimize the impact of your group on the environment. We had a simple rule we tried to follow: Leave a campsite in such a condition that the next party along will believe they're the first to use it.

Like Water Rat, enjoy your messing about, but do it with respect for the water and for the land.   RON FISHER

Library of Congress CIP Data

Fisher, Ron, 1938-
 Still waters, white waters.

 Bibliography: p. 198.
 Includes index.
 1. Canoes and canoeing — United States.
I. National Geographic Society, Washington, D. C. Special Publications Division.
II. Title.
GV776.A2F57   917.3   76-56997
ISBN 0-87044-231-7

Composition for STILL WATERS, WHITE WATERS by National Geographic's Phototypographic Division, Carl M. Shrader, Chief; Lawrence F. Ludwig, Assistant Chief. Printed and bound by Kingsport Press, Kingsport, Tenn. Color separations by Progressive Color Corp., Rockville, Md.; J. Wm. Reed Co., Alexandria, Va.